Swaziland and Soweto Revisited

Swaziland and Soweto Revisited

Lewis J. Poteet

Rock's Mills Press
Rock's Mills, Ontario • Oakville, Ontario
2024

Published by
Rock's Mills Press
www.rocksmillspress.com

Copyright © 2024 by Lewis J. Poteet.
All rights reserved. No part of this publication may be reproduced, distributed, or transmitted in any form or by any means, including photocopying, recording, or other electronic or mechanical methods, without the prior written permission of the publisher, except in the case of brief quotations embodied in critical reviews and certain other noncommercial uses permitted by copyright law. For permission requests, contact the publisher at customer.service@rocksmillspress.com.

Swaziland and Soweto Revisited is a memoir depicting and discussing historical events and the author's experiences. As such, it includes language that today would be considered hurtful and unacceptable.

"Calvin's Inadvertent Call for Apartheid (1555)" is reprinted by kind permission of the author, George Elliott Clarke.

For information about trade, library, and bulk orders, please contact the publisher at customer.service@rocksmillspress.com or through our website.

Dedication

To Nelson Rohihlahla Mandela
&
Henry Theodore Poteet

Contents

Author's Note ... 11

Timetable of Events and Dates ... 15

Opening ... 17

My First Trip to South Africa, Fall 1946 ... 19

Nurses' Residence, Bremersdorp Nazarene Mission Station ... 23

Swaziland and the Union/Republic of South Africa ... 27

Send the Light ... 30

My Lens on Three South African Landscapes ... 35

The Second Landscape ... 41

The Third Landscape ... 44

My Second Coming to the Gates of the Nazarene Hospital, November 2012 ... 47

Scottish Doctor: Samuel W. Hynd ... 49

Chief Luthuli: Confirming the Link with the Nazarenes ... 56

Missionary Son ... 58

My First Words and the Gift of Tongues ... 71

Am I Special or What? ... 78

Come See ... 83

A Small Breach in Apartheid in Nancefield, P.O. Kliptown, in 1949 ... 87

Faith of My Father: "Sacrifice!" ... 101

Scene One: Nancefield, 1950 ... 110

Scene Two: Outside Church: A Circus, A Movie, Tuck's Farm, and a British Man on Horseback ... 116

Scene Three: The Monkey Bite ... 119

Two South African Ladies ... 125

Appendix: Key Words ... 129

Postscript ... 135

Lewis-Jarrette Poteet ... 136

Lewis J. Poteet: Curriculum Vitae: "What I have done so far in my life" ... 139

Brothers in History, Brothers in Time: Henry and Frank— Melvin and Me ... 141

Brethern Dwelling Together in Unity (Not) ... 148

Anybody's Army ... 157

My Escape from the Nazarenes, Graduation Day, 1961, Bethany Nazarene College ... 159

Sex, the Swazis, and the Nazarene Saviour... 162

Where Was the Secret Meeting? (BOSBERAAD) ... 165

An Eyewitness to Black Schooling and Life in a Pretoria Township in the Late 1930s ... 169

Calvin's Inadvertent Call for Apartheid (1555)

Negroes require thoroughbred *Husbandry*—
or safekeeping (*Benevolence*)—

to uplift them from their thoughtless *Filth*,
their dodgy *Theology*—
as backward as the Devil's strut.

Pale *Prejudice* arraigns the blacks
as cockroaches of *Civilization*,
whose sacrifices of blood and breath
serve to uplift Europe's GDP
(a blessing for we Holy Roman Christ-faces)—
into (ironically) the "black."

A miraculous breed,
the Negro's *Industry* never flags
much unlike a horse's—

so we should consider these savages
God's gift to imaginative *Believers*
His own icy Caucasoids,
Us.

(The Negro's very genitals—genial—
rate many gold coins.)

We Boers are not maniacal or mean.
In *Business*, we must be as detached
as bankers weighing *Discretion*.

To exercise sovereign, vivid *Logic*,
we rate the nigger an invaluable beast.

Exuberant in his *aberrance*,
the Negro brays *Liberty*
in his uncompromising—
yes, but incomprehensible—
lungs.

[Zurich (Switzerland) 13 *décembre* mmxiii]

George Elliott Clarke

Author's Note

Though this work uses memoir and travelogue at times, I only use them to help share stories about South Africa and Swaziland that make possible a clear look at how religion, music, and the new capitalism of the post-apartheid years interacted with and finally defeated apartheid.

Swaziland, almost enclosed by the Republic of South Africa, has been a refuge from, an alternative to, a fulcrum for the larger country with which it shares so much. As a British protectorate, it was independent of, though not untouched by, the forces acting across the border. A kingdom, with a traditional clan structure, Swaziland contrasts with the diversity of South Africa: rural versus urban; religious versus secular... The interplay between these two places has fascinated me since at age six I began to notice the world around me, and did so as I lived just over two years each in both.

In 1946, six years old, I accompanied my parents, flying by Pan American World Airways from LaGuardia Airport in New York City to Leopoldville, Belgian Congo, in central Africa. Then we completed the journey by train and car, arriving at the Nazarene Mission station in Bremersdorp, Swaziland. They were starting their missionary work: Dad was in charge of the large mission farm, and I entered the first grade at the white school in the town. In 1949, the Nazarenes sent us to Kliptown, a suburb of Johannesburg on the southwest side, to build a church for the "coloured" people. We returned to the United States in 1952, by freighter, Durban to New Orleans.

Sixty years later, after working as a boy preacher, graduate teaching assistant, professor, and linguist in the American Southwest, Minnesota, and Montreal, I returned, three years running, each November, in 2012, 2013, and 2014. This book tells that story.

I tell it in parts, in two voices. The young years are in my boyhood, missionary kid voice. To try to make sense of these early stories, I talk about how I came to understand the dramatic changes I witnessed in 1946–1952, in my mature voice, with, I hope, a more balanced mind and heart.

Lewis J. Poteet
October 2023

When I was a child I saw as a child, I spoke as a child,
I prophesied as a child. But when I became a man I put away
childish things.
1 Corinthians 13:11

These fragments have I shored against my ruins.
Eliot, *The Waste Land*

Left: The author, age 4 to 6.
Right: The author, age 10, Boksburg, Transvaal.

Timetable of Events and Dates

1652: Jan van Riebeeck lands at Cape. First European beachhead, Dutch.

1835–1840: The Great Trek (Afrikaaners, covered ox wagons, prayer: the British have occupied Cape Town so decisively that the Boers seek a homeland further north. In the Witwatersrand and the Orange Free State, they declare independent Republics where they may use blacks to break the hardpan and the Boers may worship their God).

1880s: Anglo-Zulu Wars. Dingaan, warrior chief of the Zulus.
1890s First and Second Boer Wars.

1920s–30s: Nazarenes occupy Swaziland. Dr. Hynd. Harmon Schmelzenbach I.

1946: First Nazarene post-World War II infusion of new missionaries into Bremersdorp, including Poteets.

1948: Poteet and Chalfant tent revival in Kliptown establishes Nazarene coloured work.

1952: Nationalist Party victory in South Africa replaces Smuts with Malan, stiffening Apartheid. Poteets (now six in number, with Jim and Dewey added) depart Durban–New Orleans.

1955: Freedom Charter, Kliptown.

1950s, '60s, '70s, '80s: Treason Trial. Boer refinement of Apartheid: Education Act, Homelands Act, Passbook Law 1970. Detroit: Sixto Rodriguez CD of inner city Detroit music falls flat, goes gold in Cape Town.

1970s, '80s: International sanctions on South Africa. Dutch Reformed Church quits World Council of Churches. Dissident voices: Antjie Krog, at 18, first book of poetry, and Athol Fugard clandestine theatre in Grahamstown, Port E., Cape Town Swaziland casino/RSA bloodshed/ANC/Luthuli.

1990s: Bosberaad/Mandela moved, freed, elected; Sixto Rodriguez concerts in South Africa.

2012: I return to Manzini, Kliptown. Mutsepe joins Buffett Challenge. Zuma reelected.

2013 (December): Death of Mandela. Zuma booed at memorial service. My second return trip.

2014 (November–December): My final return trip—nine days in Parktown at Band B, local library.

Opening

I started to grow up in South Africa between 1946 and 1952. My mind was shaped by what I saw, heard, smelled, feared, hoped there. In grade one, in the white school in Bremersdorp, Swaziland, the hilly kingdom above the Indian Ocean, my mind was a boy's mind, as blank as the heavy paper stock of my geography workbook with the map of European and African countries in muted colours. I still have this little schoolbook, the blue cover faded and dog-eared.

I have wanted to write this book since I discovered, at about age eight, that humans wrote books too, not only God. (I learned to read because my Daddy guided me through the Bible, page by page.)

So to get ready to write, I saved:

1. A newspaper photo of the Pan Am DC-4, the "land plane" that brought me from LaGuardia to Leopoldville;
2. The watercolour painting on 1/8-inch beaverboard by cousin Nita's leper nurse pal, of Swazi hills and huts;
3. Mother's *Lessons in Zulu*, with notes in her fine round hand;
4. My own sermon notes from 1953, in Texas, in the red vinyl-covered 3 x 5 ring binder;
5. Dad's Pastor's Pocket Record of every one of his Nazarene pastoral Sunday services, Oklahoma to Swaziland.

Many of these these images appear in the pages to come.
I only began writing in early August 2012 when, sitting alone

in Brasserie Fredmir on Gouin Boulevard in Montreal's West Island, I saw clearly that the only way to do it was to *do it*.

First step was to find a phone number in San Francisco for my Johannesburg playmate Sammy Moonsamy, and my first try on Google nailed it. "Jarrette!!" he said.

Since then, two to four hours sleep a night, $57,000 Canadian for three trips to South Africa, two to Frisco, five to Oklahoma City, and a carton of paperclips and Scotch tape. And gallons of coffee.

On the aircraft in 2012 and 2013, my legs swelled, I got dizzy, and when my blood pressure spiked at 200 systolic and my pulse went down to 37, I got a pacemaker on January 11, 2014 for my body, a dog on June 7 for my soul, and five stitches in my head on December 13 in Joburg, for balance, vision, memory, and, as my cousin Jim said, after the fall, "to knock some sense into you."

The book comes out in fits and starts, in flashes. Lewis meeting Jarrette. Writing happens after an hour of fitful sleep, waking, then stammering and scribbling. I write a clear memory of an event.

My first clear flash is of riding at age six in a twenty-car motorcade of new Nazarene missionary families, through the gates of Bremersdorp Nazarene Mission Station, Swaziland. Brown people lining the stone walls are singing "Endleleni yonke kungu Jesu," a traveling song: "All the way along, it is Jesus."

Dedicated student and missionary son then, I now as a writer only trust the clear flashes. Come with me now.

My First Trip to South Africa
Fall 1946

Six years old, living temporarily at my grandmother Poteet's house in County Line, northwest Fisher County, West Texas, I received thirty immunization shots at the Sweetwater hospital, thirty miles southeast. They were against bubonic plague, malaria, tsetse flies, you name it. Six trips, five injections in my arms each trip.

We boarded the train in Sweetwater, and we disembarked in New York City. Dad took us to the basement of the Empire State Building and bought us ice cream.

At LaGuardia Airport, aboard the Pan American DC-4, I stared out the window as the taxi roll started, and asked my father how long we would be in this tube, in these seats. He said, "A week."

Next I remember, early in the morning, waking up as the pilot's voice from the intercom said "Because of fog in London airport, we will have lunch in Shannon, Ireland." Father held the strap from Steve's harness (Steve was two), and Mother took my hand, as we turned left at the front end of the narrow aisle and started to go down the portable stairs. We followed the lines on the tarmac to the terminal doors. We ate breakfast.

Stephen and Jarrette Poteet, c. 1946.

Next we were in Lisbon in a hotel for a night, then in dark Monrovia, in North Africa, for another hotel night. We left Pan American in Leopoldville, Belgian Congo.

In the hotel dining room, Dad said, "Let's have some local food. I see mealies. Let's have that."

We ate the food they brought, delicious boiled and buttered roastin' ears of corn, and then Dad asked the waiter, "Where are the mealies?"

The waiter pointed to the corn cobs.

I stared out the window, fascinated at the vast blue water lapping at the foot of the lush green yard and stretching from left as far as I could crane my neck, to as far right, and with no opposite shore in sight.

"Is that the ocean?" I asked Dad.

"No, Jarrette, that is the Congo River. It is over a mile wide here."

Next, a few days later, Dad brought boxes of ham and cheese sandwiches to our hotel room, and then we took them with our hand luggage to the airport again. This small airplane, not as orderly as the big one, was for the missionary group only, fourteen of us, and the pilots took cash. They did not wear uniforms; after they bought it, left over from the World War, they fixed it. But they took us to another city, Elizabethville, and we took a train, headed by a coal-burning steam engine that belched tiny black cinders that now and then wandered into our open passenger car window. It was hot.

Each compartment had four seats, so Father and Mother, Steve and I, had our own. Next to us were some of the Nazarene nurses, and at one switching yard, after waiting hours, I felt a gentle bump and heard big metal pieces bumping and locking in with a smooth, clunky sound. Excited, I rushed from the corridor, my guard-station, into what I thought was our compartment. But it was the next one over, and my words to the astonished Della Rogers and Miss Flitcroft and their two friends were "Daddy, we're hitched." My father found this misdelivered message, right in the faces of these celibate-for-life, married-to-Jesus Nazarene nuns, hilarious, and he embarrassed me for years telling the story to his friends.

I do not remember changing trains in Johannesburg, several days later, but Dad says we did, and only got off at the border of Swaziland.

Twenty cars met us, and we caravanned for two hours. Then, the part I remember more vividly than any other: the arrival at Bremersdorp Nazarene Mission Station.

The brick walls on each side of the massive gate, with the Raleigh Fitkin Memorial Hospital a one-story long, low whitewashed building in front of us, were lined with hundreds of brown people.

They were singing, and I remembered the words and the tune from that day on, though I as yet knew no Swazi.

Endleleni yonke kungu Jesu (repeat); *Umsindisi wami, endleleni yonke; endleleni yonke kungu Jeeessuuu.*

(All the way along it is Jesus; all the way along Blessed Jesus; He's my joy and song; all the way along; all the way along, it is Jeeeeesus.)

Like a ticker-tape parade into Heaven.

Nurses' Residence, Bremersdorp Nazarene Mission Station

Olathe, Kansas. Kansas City First Nazarene Church, on a Sunday Morning in April 1996

Standing, slightly breathless, at the Uphaus portal into the 2000-seat auditorium, banked, arcing seat rows almost full of Nazarenes at the mother church, I pause, lean against the side jamb. Everyone turns his face up to the 200-voice, blue-robed, white-sashed full Sunday Morning Worship choir, four rows deep, also arced so the two massive banks of people form a gigantic oval, the smaller bank above. From them comes the massed sound that fills the room like a a king surf wave higher than us all. Four men and several children are scurrying to their seats.

I am just ready to run out, my mission done, as the service starts. Fifty men open in rich, deep bass, "Holy, holy, holy, Lord God Almighty…" the sopranos, then the altos, then the tenors swelling the sound. I burst into tears as I run along the curving exit hallway toward the sunshine. No one is watching me, I imagine, as I turn left and swing into the open door of my Volvo, Martin at the wheel, engine running.

Kansas City First Nazarene is not where I last saw it. South of town in open suburban Olathe (Gary Hart's home town), it more resembles a Cirque du Soleil permanent tent than the somber old church in the city I remember, with its dark brick, tall steeple. That one is now abandoned to inner-city decay. KC First is where the five general superintendents worship on a rare Sunday off, at home; I came here today just to drop off one of my slang dictionaries to Connie Cunningham, who is married to one of these Nazarene "archbishops," and a kind man pointed me to the section and row where she usually sits. Not finding her, I gave them to the woman in her Sunday best who usually sits beside her, Connie's name in black marker on the envelope, and she nods as she receives it from my hand. I run.

It is too perfect, the grandest Nazarene Sunday morning opening I can imagine, and it brings back in a flood from my eyes all I have lost, in my swelling heart.

Forty years ago I last saw Connie when she and her sister Betty, closer to my age and thus my playmate in the yard between our house and theirs, and inside the house, once, memorably, just two houses down from the long white wings of the Raleigh Fitkin Memorial Hospital, the heart of our new temporary home, Bremersdorp Nazarene Mission Station, in Swaziland. Both Betty and Connie, cute and lively, were only daughters of Dr. Lauren Seaman, who had just delivered my second little brother Jim. Stephen and I were the only sons of my father, Henry Poteet, the new American with his missionary task undefined as yet. The curving gravel road from beyond their house, past ours, was lined with lush tropical trees and cacti whose names I did not know, and between our house and the hospital was the nurses' residence.

Nurses' Residence, Bremersdorp Nazarene Mission Station
"Nurses" were all young women, Americans, Scots, English, Swazi, Zulu, even Shangaan, all living together in these one-story stucco-walled four-room familiar furnished sturdy homes, Our parsonages in Hooker, Oklahoma and last in Manhattan, Kansas had been just the same size, also comfortably furnished. But here the ten or twelve buildings made up the small village of the mission station, like a living room in which aunts sat at odd angles and beamed at me (I had five). Here, gravel roads led both ways to the print shop, beyond the hospital to the old brown

stone church, and onward past the school to curve sharply left and run along a ridge out to the mission farm.

Indeed, they were like aunts to me, but all single. Dorothy Bevill, Miss Flitcroft, Dora Carpenter, Sara Munro, Elizabeth Cole—at least I remember the names of the white nurses. I even had a first cousin among them, Nita Clegg, but she was a nurse to the lepers, in the leper colony that had to be far from uninfected people, way south in Swaziland. The hapless lepers, with twisted hands and mouths, lived in huts.

Leper Colony Huts

The skyline, the thatched cones of the straw roofs on the little cupcake huts, all are familiar to me, when I look at the little painting one of Nita's fellow nurses painted, though I was never taken there, of course. They are the shapes of home, my first homeland in Africa, so different in the colours of people and flowers and trees, but so like Texas in its scrub trees on baked rolling hard ground. I am surprised at how I could fall asleep, with the enormous change, so big it felt like a rebirth. I could fall asleep, but soon I began to walk in my sleep, and wet my bed, and it ran on until I was eleven.

Leper Colony Huts, southern Swaziland.

Swaziland and the Union/Republic of South Africa

Though this writing at times uses both the modes of memoir and travelogue, I do so only to help explore the interchange and contrast between Swaziland and the South Africa republic that surrounds it on three sides. Specifically, I try to share a clear look at how religion, music, and politics destabilized and eventually defeated apartheid. To say it another way, every time in the last two months of 2012 that I crossed the South Africa/Swaziland border, I had to buy a new SIM phone card and write down a new, long phone number.

Swaziland has been a stable refuge for refugee activists from the Nationalist apartheid years (1948–1994), and as a British protectorate, it kept its traditional clan structure and monarchy; South Africa had "kings," e.g. Shaka in Zululand, but by the twentieth century the tribal structure was in the hands of chiefs, e.g. in Zululand, Chief Buthelezi; in Xhosa territory, the royal family known as Thembo, in which Nelson Mandela was an advisor to the chief.

In South Africa, power was in the hands of the Afrikaner Nationalist Party, and through very unstable years, its urbanism contrasted sharply with rural Swaziland. Much power in South Africa rested in the lucrative mining companies, extracting gold, diamonds, platinum, coal, clay; and at the election of Mandela (1994), a coalition of tribal groups, Communists, and labour unions formed a government that sought to bring justice to the aftermath of apartheid. Not entirely friendly to business, it nevertheless avoided confiscation of industries along Communist lines.

And the years of international sanctions had produced some inventive technology, for example, the extraction of liquid fuel from coal, in which the country led the world. Swaziland, though, benefited when multinational corporations' regional headquarters, such as Coca-Cola's, moved in to find stability during the bad years in the RSA. Many of them are still there.

One specific way to mirror the difference between the two countries is to consider Alexander McCall Smith's eyewitness account of a peaceful spot in Swaziland in 1980 as contrasted with the rioting, repression, and turbulence in South Africa that year, a full nine years before Mandela would be released from prison. Asked the question, "Where is the most incredible place you have ever been?" Smith's answer was Siteki, a small town in the Lebombo Mountains. The town

> seemed to have been forgotten, but ... still had an old colonial hotel [with] a dining room in which each table was carefully laid with white linen and silver. I never saw anybody else eating there. The whole town had the feel of having been left over from somewhere in the Fifties. One had the impression at any moment one might encounter the shade of a former district commissioner on his way to an evening of bridge. On the road along the ridge of the mountains, I discovered a deserted farm house. Behind, the land dropped down sharply to the low veld below, and one could look out for miles, over a landscape of shimmering heat, of browns and reds, to hills made blue by distance. I sought out the farmer who owned the house, and he walked with me round the property, he with his gun under his arm. What made this place so special? High air, Africa distilled, as Isak Dinesen would have it; a sense of loss; a sense of being missed by the world.

South Africa's success on achieving mutual acceptance across previously divided communities may hearten hope for other much-needed reconciliations today. I hope to assist this process of tolerance building through the writing of my book.

My contacts in South Africa are substantial, the most important one being Maurice Podbrey, founder of Montreal's Centaur Theatre who went on to work with a new theatre in Cape Town. Mr. Podbrey brought Athol Fugard to Montreal to direct *A Lesson from Aloes*. In his early career as a playwright, Fugard had resisted apartheid laws by staging clandestine theatre (basement) events in Port Elizabeth. Podbrey and I arranged an event at Concordia University at which Fugard answered questions in a room strangely haunted by the very smell of fear that was palpable in the years I was in South Africa. Present at the Fugard event was my second principal contact, Frank Chalk, of Concordia's Genocide Institute and professor of South African history. Frank has been an invaluable bibliographical resource, and I plan to meet with him at a conference at Pretoria University in December.

Analogous publications for comparison with my project are Richard Poplak's *Ja No Man: Growing up White in Apartheid-Era South Africa*; Daniel Coleman's *The Scent of Eucalyptus: A Missionary Childhood in Ethiopia*; and Barbara Kingsolver's *The Poisonwood Bible*, which planted the seed of my project some years ago.

Send the Light

There's a call comes ringing o'er the restless wave
Send the light, send the light.
There are souls to rescue, there are souls to save.
Send the light, the blessed Gospel light.
Let it shine from shore to shore.
 Send the light, and let its radiant beams
Light the world forevermore.

—Missionary Hymn

Why is the wave "restless"? Wind, a spirit, pushes any elevated water surface, and speeds it along, presumably from, say, Africa's west coast toward, say, the slave market in New Orleans.

The gospel light travels the other direction. Now while light travels much faster than water, it does not calm the wave, or slow, let alone stop it. It can only show the shape, height, colour. No, to calm a raging sea, oil is the thing.[1]

My father had a dream in the 1930s, that black people, a host of them, were waving, beckoning to him to come over and help them. The only help my father, a preacher, knew to offer was to try to save their souls, fairly unspecific. Other Nazarenes, Scot-

1. Gospel music travelled west to east from America to Africa. But at its core, gospel music is of African origin in rhythm and harmony. And Sixta Rodriguez' 1970 album *Cold Fact* in a single copy appeared in Cape Town and was bootlegged. Its powerful Detroit street and working class music spoke to the people suffering under apartheid, and as the movie *Searching for Sugarman* shows, helped change South Africa while for 30 years no one in South Africa knew where the singer/writer was, and he got no money. So not only gospel music crossed.

tish and American doctors, nurses, and teachers were giving specific medical help and schools.

But after two years, the mission and my father found a concrete task for him, and it became a part of the real force that took down apartheid. In Kliptown, where in 1955 the Freedom Charter was drafted, Dad did practical good: the church he built in 1949 was a meeting place for coloured and Indian people, and gave them energy to act, and the solid belief that all humans are equally valuable.

Multiplied many times over, the Kliptown Church of the Nazarene helped make possible the ANC coalition that toppled apartheid.

Boundary Road, where the church was and is, had no electricity in 1949. The church was lit by kerosene (there called "paraffin") lanterns. But the inner light, the light of warmth and freedom, was for my father's flock the Gospel light.

In 2012 a Cape Town journalist called the release of Mandela and the free election "the Dawn of Freedom." Dawn, the coming of the light. The light of reason. What Matthew Arnold meant by culture: sweetness and light.

In 2012 the Nazarenes are sending light in the very tangible form of solar-powered water pumps, over fifty so far.

> Let your light so shine before men
> that they may see your good works.

Angel Keili: What Now?
Arriving in Durban by South African Airways CRJ, I reached the Parade Hotel by shuttle.

After checking into Room 503, on the top floor, I looked out over the Indian ocean beach, with incessant even rolling waves inbound.

At the bar, Julius served me a Windhoek beer. In the bar. a sign read:

NO CREDIT/ ASIKWELETIS
NO SMOKING / AKUBHENYWA
NO SWEARING / ASITHUKI
NO [WORD NOT CLEAR] / AZIGENIIZINGANE EZENEMMYAKA
ENGAEHANSI KUKAJ 8

Looking slantwise out the door. the first serious street person, a shaggy, barefoot white man picked the garbage can. draining

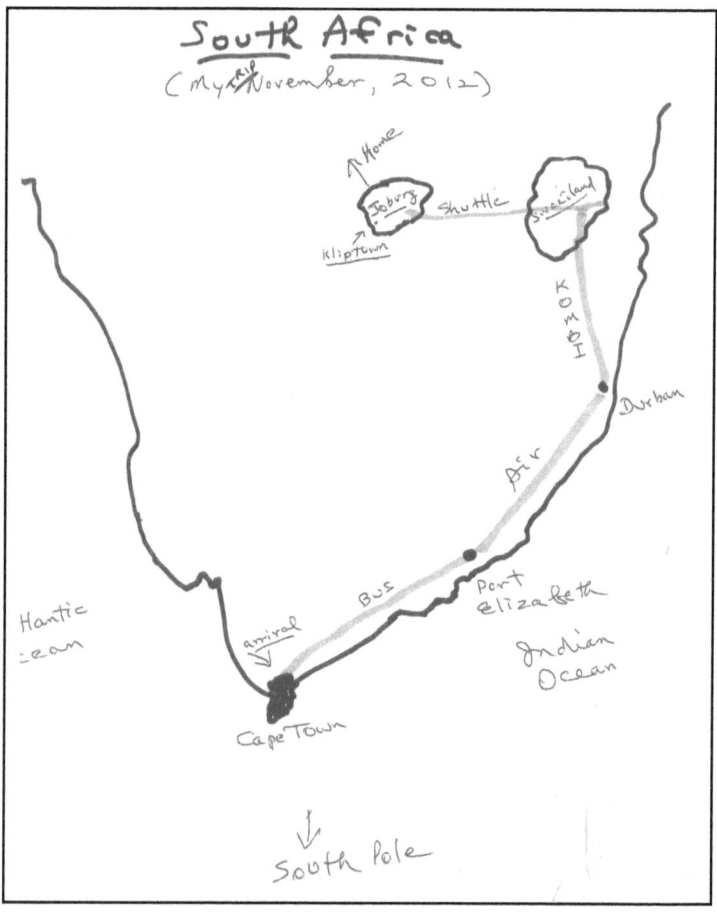

The author's hand-drawn map of his November 2012 trip.

drops of stale Coke and munching scraps. Julius said he never bothered anyone. never spoke, never panhandled, had been a regular local street bum for years.

I was not reassured. having been warned that the beachfront promenade after dark was a site of occasional knifepoint robberies. At the head of the grass strip just across the side street. beside the taxi stand. a temp trailer detention was a new South Africa Police crowd control unit, with VW-sized tanks at either end, one for M, the other for F.

The music of my aerie was the ululating drone of the surf and the melody of car and truck motors mixed with the rooftop birdsong, the edge just above my window, and the voices of passersby, clearly rising the six floors from the street.

The coffee facility in this hotel room, as in every other one, enabled easy coffee, always instant. I used it regularly from 3 p.m. till bedtime.

Breakfast, served from 6 a.m., was sumptuous, multicourse, juice, fruit, fried tomatoes, eggs any style, bacon or sausage, rolls, toast, pancakes. Now and then a thin, gaunt man would tend the griddle, and when he saw that I read the newspaper as I breakfasted, asked me if I would pass it to him when I finished. He did not eat until 1 p.m., but he had to read as he ate, like me. He was a single parent, originally from the Cape. He was Coloured. His adopted daughter, Keili, I saw tending a small child in the stairwell between the third and fourth floors. They lived on the second, in the corner apartment.

Rudi Kretsen, for that was his name, became my friend. We only spoke for a few minutes at a time, as he worked, but when on my third day I considered how to venture safely out for one evening adventure, I thought of Rudi, who worked only until about noon.

At Durban City Hall, a short cab ride from the Parade Hotel, a French troupe promised an aerial and acrobatic show, ANGEL'S PLACE; PLACE DES ANGES. Rudi agreed to go with me.

But when I went to his apartment, he was prone on his daybed, not unwell, but resting, and he said that he could not go, as he had something come up.

"Keili will take you," he gestured toward the girl I had seen in the stairwell.

"I'll bring us there in a taxi," I responded, and we were off. Sensitized as I am by the North American extreme politically correct taboos, I rode shotgun beside the driver, seating twelve-year Princess Keili in state in the rear seat.

My guide, when I asked, said that she had never been at such an event before. Her bearing was confident, and when I asked if she knew how to return by bus if necessary, she said, "Yes."

She was quiet. Her skin is a shade or so more brown than her father's. Her mother does not live with them. Her school was in Glenwood, Morningside. Her hair is black, stiff, straight. We spoke more often with our eyes than with our voices.

Leaving the cab, she led me, darting like a jackrabbit through the stream of people, down beside the City Hall, and to a seat on a concrete block wall in front. She refused any juice or soda, but shared a box of small doughnuts with me.

At seven, a procession of clowns on stilts, with twinkling electric haloes, wove through the crowd. Just after an announcement ("main event delayed a half hour"), rain began to fall. No aerial show. We streamed with the crowd toward the Royal Hotel lobby, across Anton Lambede Smith Street. As soon as we got out of the rain, I spotted a hotel bathroom, and ducked in. For half an hour in a stall I sweated profusely, wetting my clothes from the inside: the outside was already sodden. And after voiding my bladder, I pulled my togs up and my spirits together. I rejoined my little angel just outside, we walked up two blocks to the cabstand, and went back to the hotel.

My Lens on Three South African Landscapes

After five days recovering from the thirteen-hour British Airways flight from London's Heathrow Airport on an old Boeing 747, I hoped the Cape Town bus station could give me a comfy ride to Port Elizabeth, upcoast along the Indian Ocean. The East Cape from the first-class bus seat looked like a reclining, ample Mother Earth—rolling, open, fertile. Herds of cattle at their green brunch, horses in close brotherly discourse with each other and with spring offspring colts here and there; slightly off-white sheep by the hundreds, like a lake surface in Quebec during a brisk wind, the moutons (whitecaps). An ostrich farm. Vineyards with Huguenot names like "Delaire Graf Estate" and French names like "Mont Destin Wine Farm." During the twelve-hour ride, no wind, only sun and the rolling East African hills.

After a few days learning my laptop in Port Elizabeth, I flew South African Airways to Durban, on a Bombardier RJ seventy-seater.

Getting from Durban to Swaziland was not so easy. Again twelve years old in my head as I was when we in 1952 steamed out of Durban aboard the S.S. *Ruth Lykes*, New Orleans bound, I did not remember which side of the road the cars drove on, since I did not yet drive.

Trying to move on from Durban, my phone calls to the bus station did not find me a seat for Swaziland. Anoop Singh, taxi driver at the stand beside the Parade Hotel, was volubly, aggressively helpful. "I'll take you," he said. "I drove a man to the

Isandlhwana Battlefield yesterday, and we stopped by the Phezulu Safari Park on the way back. You could see the Big Five."

Baffling to me at first, Big Five was local code for Elephants, Lions, Rhinoceros, Buffalo, and Zebra. But I did not come back to Africa to do safari.1 I did know that battlefield name from a phrase in local slang to describe being deliriously happy—"as elated as the Zulu after the battle of Isandlhwana," because, guess who beat the British in that opening of the Anglo-Zulu War of the 1880s. No, I came back to retrace my boyhood steps, and Dad did not take me to battlefields. Besides, I sensed that M. Singh took me for a bwana with many Rand and a fetish for exotica. A ride in his taxi all day would cost five times my bus fare from Cape Town.

Durban, the first place I could pick up our trail from the 1940s, had been a *cul de sac* so far. In the summers of 1947–1949, Dad drove us in the 1937 Willys sedan to Durban. We stayed for two weeks at a missionary vacation home run by the Salvation Army. I remembered it well, but I had no idea how to find it. In that big old house five blocks up from the North Beach, the room next to ours housed a thin, retired nurse to the lepers whose afternoons were guarded by a sign on the door: "Do Not Disturb, Talking to Jesus." I was slightly stung by a jellyfish at the beach.[2]

I asked the taxi maestro about the home. "It is now an orphanage," he said. He did not know where it was. I asked how I could get a bus ticket to Manzini. "Greyhound," he said, and he brought me there and then back after the bus station turned out to have no bus to Swaziland. His pal from the cabstand knew how to get there, though, and next morning, Sunday, at 7 a.m., dropped me at an unlabeled parking lot north of the central post office on Dr. A. O. Zuma Street, mercifully short of the ominously named Muti Market ("muti" is curious plants and powdered

2. If you consulted this book to find exotic African wildlife, bwana, you may want to skip to the section titled "The Monkey Bite." Or, if you read on to the account a few pages further along in this section describing my luxury ride from Swaziland to Johannesburg, you will find rhinoceros.

body parts for witchcraft).

The Durban lot was almost full of various kombi buses, but my driver weaved his old Corolla through them, and at the north end we spotted the SZ plates that meant these mini-vans were licensed in my destination, the mountain kingdom between Natal and Mozambique.

Kombi lot, Durban.

Warned that the aging Savana fifteen-seater would not leave until it was full, I bided my time with cigarettes, chats with the other travelers, and a parade of vendors, selling nut bars, Durban round straw hats, and a green plastic string-and-spring assault helicopter model. I bought one. At noon the driver's sidekick finally took my fare, R 45, we piled in, and the motor started on the first try.

Towing the tiny luggage trailer, we made a grand takeoff roll, good for twenty feet. The old bus then coughed and died, and only restarted after the driver unhooked the luggage trailer so a jump-start in reverse could work.

Out of Durban at last, past Shaka International Airport, we rolled past vast cane-fields. Then groves of straight, tall trees in even rows. I asked the young man in the seat ahead of mine what they were. "Gum-trees," he said, "farmed for pulp, and fast-growing." When we saw the hulking huge pulp-mill off to the east, so distant I could not smell the familiar St. John, NB, or East Anus, QC, stench of organic chopped tree fiber becoming newsprint, we were near the Swazi border.

The lad had told me that he was Swazi. "I get off at Lavumisa, at the border," he said. I did not want to miss the chance to learn his story, so as we passed Endlingeni I asked how he came to be in Durban. I had told him that I had been a teacher, so he told me the story of his ongoing education. He wrote it out for me in three careful pages, a document of struggle, grit, and arrival. He got off at the border, home for the summer after his first, successful year in university. And at last I was in the place of my brother Jim's birth.

* * *

Mashaba Mnqobi S., a young Swazi sitting on the seat in front of mine on the kombi from Durban to Swaziland on Sunday, November 18, 2012, told me how he came to that moment, returning from his first, successful year in university. At my request, he wrote:

I was born in Swaziland in a small town called Lavumisa where my parental home was. I later left to stay at my father's work place in Mbabane the capital city of Swaziland. In Mbabane I went to a public primary school which was not that much resourced. I spent seven successful years in the primary school but I was not the best of the students.

Swaziland has a single university that accommodate +/-20,000 students but supplied by thousands of high schools with students to be. I stayed two years at home without progress in life as it was hard to get a decent job. In 2010 I left Swaziland for South Africa to stay with my Aunt. I restarted school in a public school and then I spent two tremendous years. I transformed to be one of the best performing learners and that inspired me to where I am now at the University of KwaZulu Natal. I am persuing my B.D. degree in Pedagogics.

Transfering to a South African school changed my life to see a brighter future ahead of me. Finishing school in Swaziland made my quest for success in future to a halt. The Swaz! Education system had lots of demand and gave me a basic background in English and made me shine when I started school in South Africa. The education experience I got whilst in Swaziland made me prosper and get a University and a study loan.

—Mashaba Mnqobi S.

I asked permission to include his writing as a document of progress and arrival. "Yes," he said. "Be honoured."

Mashaba Mnqobi S.

Lewis J. Poteet

The George Hotel
Manzini, SZ, 2012

Indian ocean from hotel room balcony.

> You get old
> And you realize
> There are no answers
> Just stories

The Second Landscape

Swaziland was so much like the Texas hill country that I looked for barbecue stands. Not so fertile as the East Cape, but on the other hand, not like the land around Joburg, cursed by the greedy machines of the white gold mine entrepreneurs. Central Gauteng (aka Transvaal) is a hard-packed yellow and brown moonscape. Swaziland is hilly, very green, and the main roads are smooth and paved.

Just after dark, the kombi turned downhill, left, to cross the river into downtown Manzini. At the ragged parking lot, I hired a taxi to take me to The George, the hotel the Nazarenes had told me to reserve; they sent groups every month or so to see and help in the work, staying in rooms at this oldest and best lodging in Swaziland.[3]

They had also given me names and cellphone numbers, which I began trying the next morning. Dustin and Amanda, the young couple just a year into their work as coordinators of visits and aid. Dr. Samuel Hynd, the retired Scottish Nazarene whose father had built the hospital, and who did surgery on me when I was eight. I found Dustin and Amanda, driving their rugged dusty all-wheel drive jitney along the mission station road from the farm toward the church, hospital, and gate.

They shared a potluck Thanksgiving dinner with me the next evening, their apartment full of twenty young Americans, tour-

---

3. Parking lot sign:"Not responsible for articles left therein or thereon for any cause whatsoever." A dozen hallway paintings tell fables of how zebra stripes came to be (baboon trick) and a thieving baboon who wanted cheetah fast, lion teeth, ape brain, antelope eyes, and a dog's head.

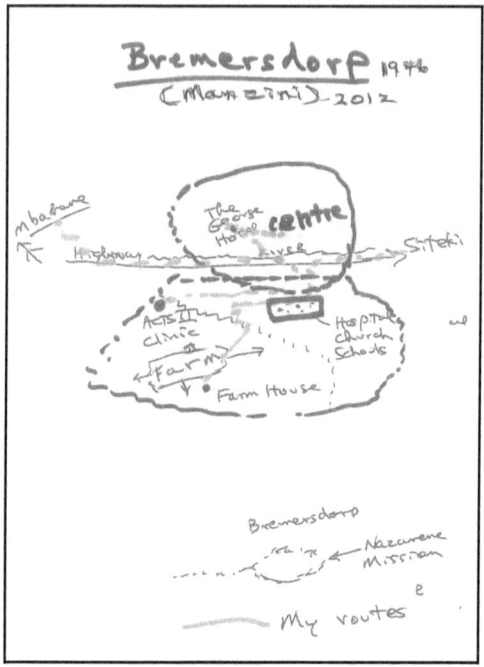

Author's hand-drawn map of Bremersdorp.

ing the world to see the mission work. A few days later, after I tired of trying to catch Dr. Hynd at his home phone (the copper wire had been stolen and he had not replaced it, I learned later), I called Dustin. On hearing my plan for the first weekend, "You want to go to Siteki?" the Swazi landscape east toward Maputo and the Indian Ocean.

Across mid-Swaziland, west to east, the main road winds from Osthoek through the capital Mbabane, past industrial Mastapha, and then slices between the grand Nazarene hospital-church-school-farm complex on the top of the hill and old Bremersdorp, just across the river. Then it runs ribbon-smooth to Siteki and Maputo. Off that road, unpaved roads rattle teeth. Rocky, cut through with gully-crossings, up and down, low spots only dangerous when it rains. That is the terrain. My teeth did a random staccato as Dustin muscled his Nissan along the side road to a Nazarene school. We were on our way, Dustin and his wife Amanda and I, to Siteki. They were working. The school, 300+ students, had asked for repairs to a leaky tin roof, and the young couple, the Nazarene "coordinators," slotted their "partnership" visit to inspect, chat, and mediate some help, during a quick stop on the way to another official visit in Siteki.

Picking me up at the hotel, Dustin had said, "We'll take you right up to Mabuda Farm B&B" with his foxlike Irish grin, "but we have to make a stop on the way."

What a stop. After a three-quarters of an hour bumpy ride, the students, from grade one to form seven, all uniformed, were marching in formation to the central hall in this large set of brick buildings surrounded by the scrub bush. The solar water pump was at one end, the Nazarene way to send the gospel light across the waves. From the back bench, I saw a morality play (Standard IV pupils), heard the Standard 11-111 chorus sing in Siswati, Afrikaans, and English. Then we ducked out ("You must take lunch," the head teacher said, handing us three boxes of chicken and fried potatoes, "to eat in the car." I waited until we were back on the main road. The kids would be fed a tasty stew, cooked outdoors between the graduation hall and the classroom with the leaky roof, stirred with big ladles in black pots over charcoal by large brown women.

We made Siteki by four, but before we reached my B&B, Dustin made another stop—more work—at the Nazarene Theological Seminary. They disappeared for an hour, I waited, and when I had to, scouted quietly in the bright sun on the empty (vacation-time) campus to find an unlocked bathroom. Coming out, I looked down the opening, descending valley the school overlooks.

This valley's twin, two miles onward, was farmed by Dr. Jonathan Pons and his wife Helen, their B&B, Mabuda, at the head of the valley. In two days in her Chalet #2 I read, out of the rain, doing my research. But when the sky began to brighten, 3:30 a.m., I used one cup of coffee to fuel me as I snapped a series of photos of the coming of the light.

The Third Landscape

Gauteng (Transvaal): First bus had been a roadworthy Greyhound, second a kombi with cracked mirror and slick tyres. The third, from the George Hotel to O. Tambo International Airport (formerly Jan Smuts), was the shuttle, late-model Twister for eight people, comfortable and fast.

After the Swazi hills, the large, rich province called Gauteng is open, vast, gently rising and falling. It is very green and fertile in the warm seasons, with herds of cattle, especially, and now and then a few rhinoceros among them, for protection from the vicious poachers who slaughter them to get the tusks. These generous large fields are watered by the latest in industrial farming technology: the long slender pipes on wheels which traverse them, spraying the vital mist, looking like some sort of gigantic alien mutant metallic insect.

But the terrain as our shuttle nears Joburg: baked clay. Afrikaner-tough, make-the-desert-bloom if you can. Brown surface there for a long time. Yellow hillocks, man-made, shaped like gigantic upside down loaves of bread. You know you getting close when you pass the huge cooling towers for a nuclear power plant, just south of the main freeway from Swaziland. And by the increasing number of those yellow loaves of slag, waste dirt from which the gold has been removed, and now and then a black one, from coal mining. More traffic, more trucks, and all going faster. The city of gold.

Opposite: Daybreak from Chalet #3, Mabuda Farm B&B, Siteki, 2012 (top.) Looking south from Chalet #2 (middle).

Swaziland and Souweto Revisited

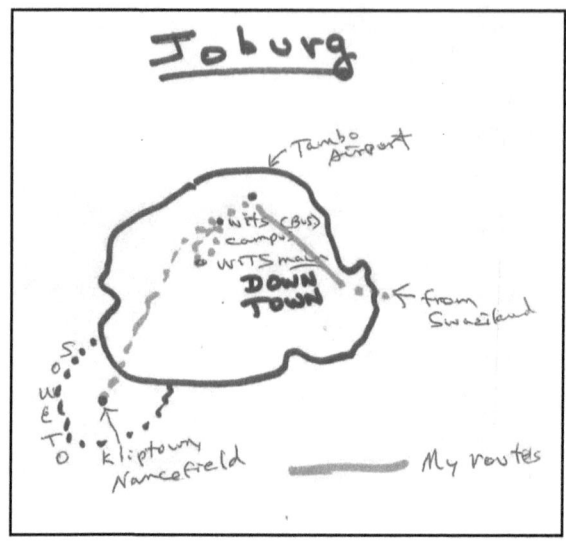

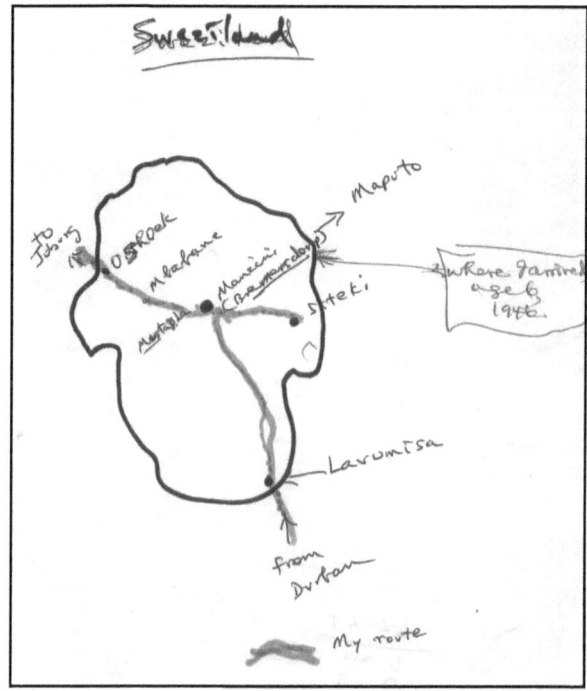

Author's hand-drawn maps of Joburg and Swaziland, showing his travels

Bremersdorp Nazarene Mission Station. This photograph was taken in November 2012. The white building (left side of the photo) is the hospital. Further left and not visible is the nurses' residence. To the right, not visible, is the old church.

My Second Coming to the Gates of the Nazarene Hospital, November 2012

From the George Hotel, I take a cab, and ask him to take me to the Hospital. Though I lived here for three years as a boy, from 1946 to 1949, I have no clue which way to walk. I had asked, "To the Nazarene mission, is it too far to walk?"

"Yes," said the gate guard, "uphill and far," and so I bid for the Manzini cab, a Toyota Corolla knockoff with a South African name, driven by Nquobi Dhamini who turns out to be a Pentecostal fervent believer. I only find this out when I try my remembered Swazi, using the words with which my father ended every prayer, "I bosisa e gamene lika Jesu Christu, umsindisi wame," "We pray in the name of Jesus Christ, our Saviour," sending him into an orgiastic weeping fit of religious fervor.

But he knows the road to the hospital, right through the old downtown, and then up toward the brow of the hill that overlooks the little city. As we get near, I spot the gates, and say, "Stop! I walk from here." I pay him the 30 emalangeni cab fare, about $2.50, and scramble out the left side. I am in tears.

Scottish Doctor: Samuel W. Hynd

Doctor Hynd on the south side of the clinic.

I first met Samuel Hynd at his medical clinic, Acts II, a new brick one-story with welcoming open portico, its roof angled upward, sheltering the concrete benches for waiting. Clean paved surround, geese feeding on new lawn, it tops a ridge overlooking New Village, just outside Manzini, Swaziland's largest city. The week I spent finding him was not due to his hiding out; his duty was just to be available daily to the people who needed AIDS medication or injections to help their knees walk the African hills. And at his house, stolen copper telephone wire was not replaced, so that my daily phone calls only seemed to tell me, in my ignorance, that he had no answering machine. Eventually I learned that I should go to his clinic, but understood so imperfectly how far it was and even which direction, I set out walking in the wrong direction and had to be headed off by the woman from the Nazarene book store and put aboard the first of two local minivan buses, where after a short hike, I saw his building.

Tall and clear-eyed, 88 years old but with no noticeable stoop, he shuffled out between patients, not even informed I was waiting, shook my hand, heard me say "I am Lewis Jarrette Poteet," and said, "This clinic is on the far edge of the farm your father ran." He remembered Henry and Ruby Poteet by name, and mother's skill on the piano. He was tall and broad-shouldered, healthy and keen of mind, a man who had not neglected to pay attention to anything that had come his way in his years, from being brought to Swaziland as a six month old infant to his eminence as the medical doctor for King Sobhuza and the next king, MsWati 111, five years of service as Minister of Health to the Kingdom, and his final project, the clinic.

Only male child of Dr. David Hynd, who did surgery on me when I was eight, in the hospital he had built onthe hill above Bremersdorp (Manzini now), his son Dr. Samuel Hynd had become doctor to the Swazi royal family, present at the bedside when Sobhuza died, birthing doctor for the current king Mswati Ill. "I am the only man in Swaziland who has swatted the king on the buttocks," he told me with an impish smile. This precise Scottish Nazarene physician is the second generation of Hynds in medical missionary service in that place (now there are four—David, Samuel, his daughter Elizabeth, and Elizabeth's daughter). He has, remarkably for a doctor, a tiny, precise, legible handwriting, and, for a Nazarene, not a word of unctuous religious cant. He took two afternoons off to drive me around and talk. On the first, he almost mired his car to the hubcaps returning on a rutted road from taking me to see the ruins of the farmhouse where we lived in 1946, '47, and '48; on the second, he was flagged down by radar police just below the mission station, for speeding; but when the officer walked up to the right-hand (driver's side) window, he said, "Take it easy, Dr. Hynd." One does not ticket the king's doctor.

Fragment of note from Doctor Hynd to author, and photograph of the old church.

Our longest talk, and best, was the last. Sitting in his Mazda 6 beside the Raleigh Fitkin Memorial Hospital, on the side near the emergency entrance, looking directly at the old stone church where I had as a boy worshipped every Sunday, we agree that the broken windows must be repaired when money comes; long ago, buttresses added stability to the mud-grouted stones. He points to the sharp short mountain above and to the left a mile up from the old church.

"I was four," he says, "and I watched the ox-teams, the king's taking the stones down from his mountain, and ours bringing them here. The king knew that the ox-teams had different parasites and infections, and so his could not come down to the mission station." He sorts out for me the colour-coding of the uniforms, robes, frocks, of the student nurses, teacher trainees, and theological students who pass us in twos and threes on every side. The unpaved road bends around the church, and goes straight west for a hundred yards, toward the farm. When

I lived there, riding my Raleigh bicycle from the school bus that dropped me in front of the hospital, I once peered into the undergrowth beside me, and looked directly into the eyes of a green mamba snake, standing on its tail. Not for long, though: I ditched my bicycle and ran all the way back to the safety of the hospital.

"The nurses' training school classroom building [three stories of plain steel and glass] was funded by money from the Swiss government," he said, "and the new wing on the hospital by Pepsi-Cola," and I sensed he had traveled to raise the money for both.

The stunner, for me, came without warning, as we paused, boys again reminiscing. "Chief Albert Luthuli," he began, and my scalp tingled, Luthuli, the Zulu anti-apartheid activist in Mandela's ANC, "when he had to seek refuge from the secret police and the Bruderbond, came and stayed here."

"I have my link" flashed through my front brain. The Nazarenes had no Desmond Tutu, but their churches and schools helped diverse people of Natonalist-era South Africa to meet, so that Nelson Mandela could bring together Zulus, Xhosa, Cape Coloureds, liberal whites, some communists, some priests-together, to topple the Afrikaner system and let freedom dawn, as one Joburg journalist called the events of 1992, releasing Mandela from prison, unbanning the ANC, and giving every South African, for the first time, the vote. And the Nazarenes gave asylum to Chief Luthuli.

And what did I give him? When he left me the second day at the George, Manzini's hotel, he recalled playing toy trucks with the son of the District Commissioner, in what is now the parking lot, but then was the front yard of the British authority's home. He told me how he met his first wife, and his second, and how they died. His mother, Agnes Sharpe Hynd, was the daughter of George Sharpe, from the United States, who brought, he said, "the holiness movement to Scotland." George Sharpe ended his days Superintendent of Nazarene Missions in Africa, Asia, and the Near East.

Fluent in Siswati, his first language, he had been sent to school in the capital Mbabane, to learn English.

I joked that as his father had so expertly wielded the scalpel on my eight-year-old body, I ventured the South African trip despite an advanced small hernia. I knew what to watch for, and if it flared up into a crisis, I knew who could fix it. By the time I returned for the second visit, in 2013, my "small" hernia had been repaired, and my surgeon told me that it was by no means small. As the repair was made by grafting a small piece of sailcloth-like material over the incision, I had no worries, since I have been a sailor, six hundred times putting out to sea (or to bay, fully three-quarters of the time), in my O'Day 19-foot craft, and returning without loss of life or injury, in Cape Negro bay, Port Latour Bay, Barrington Bay, and from several docks from Boulanger Yacht in Lachine to the public wharf at Ste.-Anne-de-Bellevue to Pointe Calumet Boat Club to Hudson Yacht Club to Oka Yacht Club to a small dock at Pointe Fortune, Quebec, just below the Carillon Dam. The latter was very nearly the worst choice of tie-up spots I ever chose, since a massive discharge of water from the opening of the dam gates raised the water level by a foot and a half, and I had to flee downriver in a panic, accompanied by my trusty first mate, Martin Stone, co-author of our two aviation slang books, and a friend from Nova Scotia, Michael Keefe, who had moved to Montreal. I mention him only because when we arrived at the safe haven of the Hudson Yacht Club, downriver, having scooted before the vigorous west wind for two hours, I shoved the tiller to port to turn in to the club docks, but I forgot to uncleat the mainsail, and the wind heeled us over so far that Michael Keefe claimed that his toes had gotten wet.

But I digress.

On the second South Africa safari, Dr. Hynd collected me at

the George Hotel, and surprised me. He said, "I am going to take you to meet my daughter."

Dr. Elizabeth Hynd, I knew, ran an orphanage for children who were adrift because of the AIDS epidemic. It was in a village between Manzini and Mbabane, named "Bethany," which I knew because in my search to contact Dr. Samuel, I had found her name and phone number in the local telephone book. "Bethany" is the name of the Nazarene college in Oklahoma from which I had graduated in 1961, named for the suburb of Oklahoma City in which it is the largest industry, directly across from the two blocks of stores which make up the "downtown." My parents graduated from it in 1938, or rather Dad did, and mother had done three years of study.

Well, I rode along toward the orphanage, on the left side of the car, and never saw a village named Bethany. When we reached a turn-off toward Dr. Elizabeth's fiefdom, a sign saying "New Hope" signaled the winding gravel and mud road up a fairly steep hill. At the top, several buildings, dormitories, school rooms, offices, and a solar water pump.

Dr. Elizabeth is a personable woman of a certain age, a parent, and a doctor of psychology, I believe, not of medicine. She took us on a tour: triplets about two years old, but the schools go through high school years, so the place is sizable. And as we bid her farewell, I mentioned my years at the Nazarene college, and said that I had not had an easy time of it.

"I discovered in my junior year that I liked the taste of beer," I said, sheepishly.

"I expect they did not like that," she said, with a slight smile.

She sometimes travels to the U.S. and Canada to raise funds for her operation. She made it easy for me to buy the book about her father's life, *Footprints on African Hearts and Lands*. And when he passed away, in August 2016, she sent me word with an email within a day of the event. A few weeks later, I asked her by email from whom her grandfather and her father received their

OBEs and CBSs, and in what years, and commented that she had big boots to fill. She replied that she could not do that, as she was "just a woman."

My last visit, in 2014, I saw Dr. Samuel but only briefly. He had his driver bring him by my hotel, and he had on suit and tie, returning from a visit to Piggs Peak, in northern Swaziland. When I later followed this contact up with an excursion to his house, also on a winding, muddy road east of Manzini, I found him in bed, just getting ready to dress to be taken to the Raleigh Fitkin Memorial Hospital for an IV ("I have been off my feed for a few days," he said, as his driver Mandia Dhlamini and I took his arms and helped him out to the car). "I am coming home after I get the IV," he said, and joked with me all the way into town.

Chief Luthuli
Confirming the Link with the Nazarenes

In Swaziland we were (on an 'unadvertised visit') guests of my wife's youngest brother's family, and pleasantly associated with the missionaries at the Nazarene Mission near Bremersdorp. Here, to our great surprise and pleasure, the Swazi Paramount (Sobhuza II) called on us, a short formal visit and an unexpected honour.

I found Swaziland pleasantly free—a welcome contrast to a country plagued with raiding police.

—Albert Luthuli, *Let My People Go* (McGraw-Hill, 1962, p. 161.

No wonder. Writing around 1960, about five years after the Boers passed the retrograde Bantu Education Act, Luthuli shows it as it is, a shameless plan to keep his people backward: the Minister "refused … one word of thanks to the missionaries, who initiated all social services among Africans (education, health…)."

AN EMAIL

To: Elizabeth Hynd
Subject: News story in Toronto *Globe and Mail* about AIDS in S Africa
The story reports on the effort by healers in Eshowe, which I believe is somewhere toward Swaziland from Durban, and it got my attention with: "in the whole KwaZulu province the 90–90–90 target for detection, treatment … etc. of HIV–AIDs has nearly

been reached. It seems to me that I heard or read that target figure formula when I visited Manzini in 2013, and your father invited me to come to the AIDS Day event at ACfS II, then when he was unable to come himself, he sent Mandla Dhlamini, his driver, to convey me there. It was one of the standout days in all my visits. My understanding of the Swazi language, fluent when I was a boy, has almost totally been swamped, so that I could grasp few words, but the day was so dramatic and open and friendly, with song, drama, speech (preachers and activists and exhorters), costume (a Swazi member of Parliament in the draped bright clothing, who of course conversed with me in English), that the day was dear and unforgettable. I was given a tee-shirt to help me souvenir, as the Frenchman says.

Very few days pass without my thinking of Dr. Samuel Hynd, who became like an older brother or uncle or mentor to me in the course of our conversations over those three years, 2012–2014. And of course, Dr. Jono saying to me immediately after that August 18 when he left us that I was one of the last links left between the beginnings of Nazarene missions and today—well, that got my attention and galvanized my will to press on with my writing on the book I have projected. I have now provisionally titled it: *"Voetsek, Apartheid": Revisiting My Early Years in Swaziland and Soweto.* I hope to send you a printed copy one day not too far off.

Does Swaziland have a report that is as heartening as the one I quoted for KwaZulu Natal? You and your father have been on the front line in this effort.

Warmly, and with such good memories of your generosity and kindness to me when we met, I remain,

Lewis J. Poteet
Montreal, Quebec, Canada

Missionary Son

April 26, 1999
Yesterday, sitting in Westmount Park waiting for the Spring Concert of the Westmount Youth Orchestra to start at newly renovated Victoria Hall, I wrote in a small notebook:

Desperately lonely. Empty life as I perceive it. Useless. Simplest tasks—maintenance of self and life—dog, car, house, food clothes—only, occupy me. The rest is anxiety sometimes to the point of panic attack, fret, worry, contemplation, an occasional movie or concert or exhibit or the very limited time with Cassie (Catherine Chase, my lady). Only with Cassie or other friends do I get relief from my head, my mental self-torture. I am told it is a symptom of depression and will pass. Often I am told "get a job, discipline and organize the time." But I worked to (early) retirement—what is retirement if it must be filled with work? I do not have the initiative within me, or cannot reach it, to seek a job. What I have done mainly for almost forty years is to teach and write. The writer's life is notoriously a lonely one. But it is a life I can do, and affirm. One thing is sure this miserable state cannot last. I worry about everything—money, driving, health use of time, loss of power to read, even to write, to socialize, to give, to love. Sometimes, to live.

I found, somewhere, from Annie Dillard, I believe, "the God of my socialization is one that punishes and covenants, the one that will abandon us if we sin. ... And some people struggle with the weight of that kind of God." I am one such. Born to Fundamentalist Christian minister parents, who took me for five years to South Africa where they were missionaries, I went to the church college, saw a wider world, and shook, I thought, the religion off. Now I am not so sure.

So it is that I am doing what I am doing now. I am writing in order to fill the time, to give some point to my existence, to emerge from my depression, to perhaps make money, but primarily to reveal and share my extraordinary experience, and through that process to recover and triumph, release my talents and powers.

First, I have, mostly not entered in any computer file, some dozen of autobiographical essays. I think they must be revealing of some of me, at certain times, and even the difference in perspective from their writing to now may itself be valuable.

I believe the first was called "My Fake Conversion." It is undated, but I guess it was drafted in fairly complete form around 1984. After it was drafted, I sent a copy to Gary Hart. When I was in college, he was an admired and emulated upperclassman. He was already back in Colorado, having not succeeded in winning the Democratic nomination for President.

The text:

My Fake Conversion

I do not have a particularly good memory for connecting events in my life with the proper calendar year. As a Ph.D. in English, I can connect author and title of many books I've never read; but I can't give you the date of the Beatles' release of *Sergeant Pepper* or *Rubber Soul*, though they were landmark events in my emotional history. But the exact date of my fake conversion has never left me: it was in mid-December, halfway through my final year of college, in 1960.

It stands out all the more remarkably because it was the last of some hundreds of religious conversions in my life, and the most profound, if indisputably the most perverse and at the same time, by a curious paradox, the most honest act of my life to that point.

For it was a fake from start to finish, a staged event, and it achieved its devilish purpose.

As a preacher and missionary's son, I was early aware of the importance of "getting right with God" in my parents' culture. Long before I reached the "age of accountability," I had seen innumerable people respond to the altar calls which ended every Sunday night service at our fundamentalist church, the Church of the Nazarene, in the little towns my father served as pastor all over Oklahoma, Kansas, and Texas. And for five years (between the ages of six and eleven—1946 to 1952) I bad seen my father work this magic on black and coloured people in South Africa, as a Nazarene missionary. I had once publicly and many times privately confessed my sins, prayed for forgiveness, and gotten up from my knees feeling cleansed and refreshed. In fact, I now see that I had become emotionally addicted to this catharsis, so that I depended on a cycle of sin and repentance for my pattern of feeling, even if the "sin" was almost always private, inevitable, and biological in origin, having to do with a healthy puberty.

Truth was, I had become a preacher myself. After we returned from Africa, travelling with my father as he raised money for the mission field in special services across the American Southwest, I found myself asked to speak to children in Sunday School classes about Africa. And I quickly developed a set of notes and a few talks, in which I would describe some of the things I remembered as a white missionary child (for example, the green maniba snake that once looked me in the eye, beside the road, causing me to throw down my bicycle and run a mile to call Dad). I would sing a song in Afrikaans or Zulu, recite the Lord's Prayer in Swazi (the local dialect of Zulu), and finish up with a tearjerker story about poverty or superstition in that land more gripped by real evil (apartheid and more) than I at that time could even comprehend.

I was, in that little pond, enormously successful. Even after my father had been let go by the mission board, and his fundraising travel across the U.S. curtailed, I was invited to hold forth at special "Youth and Missions" services across the Southwest. I would travel by bus or train, stay with the pastor of the host church, and enjoy the prestige my father had lost. Sunday dinner was invariably fried chicken (the "preacher bird"), sometimes at the parsonage and sometimes a huge spread, outdoor dinner on the grounds, with jello salad, sweet potatoes with marshmallows in them, and pie. I was paid by a free-will offering, which was mine to keep; Dad's had been deposited in an account at church headquarters in Kansas City, to pay for new equipment if he returned to Africa. And along with my sermon notes, I still have my account books, little ledgers in which I kept track of every penny, even for candy bars and cokes at bus stations. At one memorable weekend service in Denison, Texas, my appearance drew 300 people. I enjoyed the felicitous company of a fat, flirty woman seat-mate on the way back from Tucson, on the bus, to El Paso. I had special "cut" metal engraved blocks of my photograph to send for advance publicity in local newspapers. Dad bought me a new suit in Sweetwater, Texas. I rode the Santa Fe railroad to West Texas, and the Katy (M-K-T-Missouri, Kansas, and Texas railway) to Kansas. Once, I held a week of "youth revival" in Tucson, Arizona—it was on that bus ride that I felt the touch of the real world—the sexy lady I talked with on the bus. My father was immensely proud, though of course he did not know all. The whole week of revival was a sexually alive time for me, privately.

So it was that when I went to my father and mother's old college, Bethany Peniel College in Bethany, Oklahoma, in 1957, I quite naturally declared Religion as my major, even though l had been tempted by Chemistry. But I was quickly disillusioned by discovering that most of my male classmates were also religion majors, and many had had experience. I was no longer unique. And the way many of them talked about their work for the Lord was terribly unsettling to me. They bragged frankly about how much money they made. They seemed not serious about the doctrine or souls saved. One of my roommates classified churches into "good payers" or not; he and another sometime roommate teamed up, taking turns leading the singing and preaching and doubling their money. He was, within two years, kicked out of the college, for marrying, secretly, his hot little girlfriend; and within six months he was back in town for a visit, driving a Cadillac that had been given him by the grateful congregation of the big Assembly of God church in Atlanta to which he had become minister. I was sickened by all of this.

And the more I read, in philosophy and literature, the more I was convinced that the world did not run by the rules we bad been taught. I lost my faith, without saying so to anyone. My models became cynical or passionate upperclassmen, scholars, and men of the world. One of them was Gary Hart (then Hartpence), as I have suggested, a senior when I was a sophomore.

My marks were always high, and I moved easily into a Philosophy major, then on into English. I became editor of the campus newspaper and a member of the campus Kiwanis club, Literary society, and Honor society. And, away from campus, I sought out the experience I had always denied myself in the real world. Breaking every rule in the campus handbook except the one against marrying without permission, I went to movies and drank Mogen-David red wine, beer, and malt liquor, on back roads, leaning against the car. I tried unsuccessfully to lose my virginity. And after the last issue of the campus paper I edited came out, at the end of my junior year, Vernon Snowbarger, the Dean of Students, a Christian sociologist with a shit-eating grin he never took off, called me in, told me what he'd heard about what I had been doing, grimly grilled me about my off-campus sins, broke me down, and expelled me from school.

It took me a month after coming home for the summer to tell

my parents what had happened. Though I had fleeting impulses to throw myself in front of a car on the highway, I was also just well-informed enough to know that the world was not shaken by the deposition of the campus newspaper editor at that sanctimonious, self-important little school. My father got me back in on probation, and I knew I could finish my degree without losing any time; but my credits for the junior year would be in suspension during the first term of my senior year, the exact time when I needed to show off my good record to scholarship-granting boards, like the Danforth, which liked religious colleges and paid all the way through the Ph.D. I was condemned to do graduate school as a teaching assistant, a drudge, and at times I wasn't sure I'd get even that miserable subsidy. But with clenched teeth I returned for my final year.

In a calculated gesture of public self-humiliation I hired on as washer of pots and pans in the campus dining-hall kitchen, the honors student wearing sackcloth and ashes. The English Department soon caught onto my act, and rescued me, hiring me to mark papers. But as the end of the first term drew near, and the meeting of the college board at which they were to decide to reinstate my credits, I found myself nervous. I needed to do something dramatic to ensure my escape from that mean little world.

I found myself thinking of one of my old roommates' more cynical speculations. He had said, "Wouldn't it be fun to break loose, do anything you like, and after you'd made a notorious reputation as a heinous sinner, stage a fake conversion?" There was general shocked denunciation of this idea among even our circle, but he chuckled over the dramatic impact it would have, knowing well that "there is more rejoicing in heaven (and in any Church of the Nazarene) over one sinner that repenteth than over ninety and nine that need no repentance." We had both preached on that text; it added considerably to the allure of sin and consequently had great entertainment value.

"It'd never work. They'd know you were faking it," one sophomore said. But I wasn't sure. I had never been an actor, and my conversions had almost never been public, and I had never before been any kind of open sinner, but I was relentlessly drawn to the idea. So it was that, when the end of term campus revival meeting came, I deliberately stayed away until the last night, saying to myself that if I did it earlier, I'd have to attend the rest of the week. Then, the final service, I sat near the center of the congregation, on the main floor, and listened to the sermon with rapidly increasing pulse. The preacher was an old religion professor (my Greek teacher), Dr. Willie Noble King, said to have been a French Canadian(!), holder of the degree Doctor of Sacred Theology (S. T. D.), by reputation an avid reader of Greek poetry in Greek, and by the wildest of sheer coincidences, a lodger in my Uncle James and Aunt Maggie's house in the town. There was a rumor around that Dr. King, who was a lifelong bachelor and quite odd, had had himself castrated, to mortify the sins of the flesh, following the Old Testament commandment "If thy hand (etc.) offend thee, cut it off, for it is better to enter the kingdom of Heaven handless than to burn forever, etc." He was actually a charming, well-read, passionate preacher and I regretted the accident of history that had put him in that place that night. But 1 carried through my plan. After waiting a few minutes of the extended appeal we knew as the "altar call," a sort of talking blues with songs like "Tell Mother I'll be There" and a highly dramatic feeling-full voice-over by the preacher urging sinners to come forward, I slipped out of my seat and threw myself down at the altar.

As I had expected, I caused a minor sensation. Ten or fifteen people knelt around and behind me, those close enough putting their hands on my head and back, all praying loudly "Put your all on the altar!"—"Take hold of the horns of the altar and don't let go till you get through!"—"Lord, help this boy!" My eyes tightly shut, I mimed a desperate sinner breaking down, and after a reasonable time had elapsed, stood up, wiping away crocodile tears to their "Praise the Lord's"

Did it work? Well, it marked the end of my involvement with the church, with my caring either way. My credits were duly restored, and I was awarded a teaching assistantship at the University of Oklahoma; so that the next summer I was in Norman, thirty miles away, happily drinking beer at the tavern just off-campus and taking in the Wednesday night fifteen-cent movie at the Sooner Cinema, enjoying the forbidden pleasures for which BPC (by this time BNC) had given me such a thirst. But the night of my pretend prostration, after I had gone to bed, my old friend George Kline came in my bedroom, without turning on the light, and cautiously asked, putting his hand on my upper bunk headboard, "Were you … was that … you weren't really, were you?" I had to reassure him that no, I wasn't, I hadn't. And after graduation, five months later, one of the professors I bad some respect for, a psychologist, Dr. Forrest Ladd, stopped me gently as I was putting away my cap and gown and said, "I hope you someday like us better than you do now." It was a kind, if so far fruitless, gesture.

In fact, I have only one reservation about the whole event. The next day I learned that, on seeing me go down, Janice Brechbill, a very bright biology major, a free spirit (she had let my old roommate Paul Durham finger-fuck her once on the band bus), on looking down from the balcony saw me go and said "My God, if he's going, so am I." And she did. I do not know what became of her, but if she's stuck in some frame parsonage, chained to some pinhead preacher, because of what I did, then I have, in a strange sense, her life on my soul.

* * *

Some reflections: Obviously I feigned, when I wrote this, an indifference I did not and do not feel. I felt anger, and I still do, at the place, the treatment, the subterfuge I felt necessary. I am sure it coloured my life and behaviour. When I began to prepare for this large writing I am now doing, I set out some questions, and one of them bears on what I have just acknowledged. I asked, "Why do I have a fierce anger at what I perceive as being cheated, taken advantage of? Is it related to my inability (or even-often-to understand) being teased?" After all, these are very common human experiences.

I had lunch with Dr. Ladd a few years ago, and asked him why I still felt the anger. He suggested that there are, in any life, "teachable moments," times when we imprint or fix something which becomes very difficult to change or discard.

I feel a distinct pride, as I write this, in what I did.

April 27, 1999

On rereading, I was more aware of the pride I mention, even a kind of conceit, in what I took to be my cleverness.

Looking for the typed texts of the essays on my life, I found many fewer on first and second searches than I know I wrote. And the exhilaration of starting this writing has given way to a doubt that it can matter. The doubt, the paralysis, is precisely what I am setting out to defeat. Two other preliminary questions bear on it: 1. Why have I been, at different times in my life, so daring, risk-taking, and at others, very fearful and paralyzed, indecisive? And 2. Why have I mostly chosen, in my most widely noticed work (the slang dictionaries), to collect others' words more than writing my own? What effect did this have on my teaching, which ended with several years of self-doubting anxiety, though many good students reported to me and others that they found me stimulating and effective? I know that one quick answer is that I sought far more to elicit my students' responses to texts than to generate large and dominant responses of my own.

Another note that led up to this writing is another question: what have I been proud of, felt that I willed and accomplished? I found these, to start: 1. My three years of energetic work on the English department at Concordia University's External Committee, in which I organized readings and lectures from outside. 2. My books—the six slang dictionaries. 3. Discovering and exploring sexuality after a late start. 4. Teaching.

A more recent note: in myself I have come to see what seemed at first radical contradictions, irresolvable impulses and attachments, but which I am trying now to see as complementaries, dialectics: home versus travel, not having versus having—I do possess oceanfront Nova Scotia land and house, a frisky O'Day sailboat—together versus separate. Each of these is to be seen in the widest possible context in my life.

Take the first: I went to twelve schools in eleven years before college, and my parents did not own a house until long after I had left, but I desperately wanted a place of comfort and continuity, to the point where I had a recurring dream, many, many times, of a house, always from inside it, always spacious.

Yet I travelled, as a child, halfway around the world, and lived in a different city each year until I went to college. I changed schools each time I took a degree. I cannot count how many lodgings we used. Then I stayed in the same job, in the same city for thirty-one and a half years, and I am still in it. In this city, I have lived in Westmount (two different houses), in Montreal West, Pointe St. Charles, Snowdon, Laval sur le lac, and now Roxboro, for periods of from 23 years to less than one. And for vacations or research, I have travelled to Mexico, Europe, Nova Scotia, the Eastern Townships of Quebec.

And even recently I have found travel an immense relief in times of low spirits, conducive to writing, productive of adventure more than of trouble, and I looked forward to retirement, somewhat unrealistically, as a time when I would do a lot of travelling. So far I have been to Austin, Texas, with the relatives, for one month. And I am just now holding off on concrete planning for a weekend car trip to Toronto, a Vancouver fly-on-points, a sail on Gary Geddes' ocean-going boat, a Nova Scotia annual trek, and others (I must add, writing much later, in June of 2001, that I have also gone to Cuba for two weeks, and spent two winters in Austin, one of them teaching). What the hell is going on?

May 4, 1999

Just watched *Good Will Hunting*, and was very touched by his inability to decide what he wanted. I am trying to paste into this document my "Am I Special?"and am having trouble getting it in place.

May 25, 1999

Finally back to the writing, in a state of fear and trembling. The paste of that prideful partial document "Am I Special?" did work, sort of, though the meld seems imperfect and baffles me at this point. But I am pressing on with the writing, because non-fiction has always been my mode. I do not lie, and I do not make things up. The only "fiction" I have composed is a curious document called "Why People Tell Stories," and it will find its way into this writing, I am sure. It was composed in loneliness and pain, as I feel now, though for different reasons, and it is revealing. But I have never been drawn to the making of imaginary word-worlds. As I have said, mostly I have published the words of others; there needs to be a balance. These are my own words. This is my own life.

My earliest memories are of visits to the Poteet family farm near Rotan, in West Texas, by car, probably a Model T or A. Tiny Grandmother, less than five feet high, was head of the farm, my grandfather Poteet having died just before I was born. I had no idea how bleak and dry the Fisher County, West Texas land was; it was all I knew; it was semi-arid. But Grandmother had made a life there, and raised nine children (of thirteen born) to adulthood. Only Uncle John, lifelong bachelor, lived with her still, in the early 1940s when I first visited (I was born June 21, 1940). I remember a wheel rolling off the car in which we were travelling to Grandma's, and I remember sleeping on the front porch in a big double bed, the lights of oil-drilling rigs winking in the distance, in a big double bed with Uncle John, who also taught me dominoes and horseshoes, and hell, pitching washers. I remember the shower which was behind a shed, a barrel filled with water and no doubt heated only by the sun: I surprised my young mother emerging once, unbelievably beautiful, naked. I remember learning how to play horseshoes in the front yard, and dominoes in the front room. I remember the cookie jar in the kitchen. I remember the cistern just outside the kitchen door, filled by a water truck or the rare rain, and accessed by a bucket on a rope, to fill a container in the kitchen. The water was cool; the air was invariably hot.

It is strange to me how comforting it is to try to remember details of this time, which must have been uncomfortable in some ways. But in childhood we accept what is there. Church was a plain tabernacle five miles away, almost to Clegg Valley (Longhorn Valley, I believe it's been called), where my Aunt Narcie and her husband Mr. Clegg (J. Frank, but she even called him Mr. Clegg, as be was twenty years older than she). The tabernacle had sides that were raised and propped up on poles, to let any breeze through. It had as I recall a concrete floor and wooden seats. We had Sunday School and church there on Sunday. Each Sunday morning, the men would go into first and make sure there were no snakes to run out before the women and children entered. The preachers, when there was one, were circuit-riding itinerants.

In 1946, we went to Africa, but spent several months at Grandmother's to prepare for the trip. I believe it was from there that we went to hospitals in Rotan or Sweetwater to get the immunization shots, lots of them, for the trip. We went by train to New York City, then ate ice cream in the basement of the Empire State Building, flew out of La Guardia on a Pan Am Constellation of which I have a colour xerox of a January 19, 1946 inaugural photo of the flight La Guardia–Gander–Shannon, Ireland–Lisbon–Dakar, and terminating in Leopoldville, Belgian Congo. We did it in summer. The Congo was unbelivably wide, the train to Johannesburg burned coal so that cinders flew into the open windows in the steamy heat, and the car convoy welcome to Bremersdorp ended in a welcome along the roadsides and walls that was like entering Heaven.

My First Words and the Gift of Tongues

Dr. Samuel Hynd, the Scottish Nazarene doctor I met in Manzini in late November, 2012, told me that he learned English at school in Mbabane; his first language was Siswati. I too only learned proper English after I had first acquired a "foreign" or "alien" tongue.

"Jabet," my baby pronunciation of my middle name, looks strange, but I was trying to say "Jarrette," as I was called until I entered high school. It is a name not unknown in America, where I was born. Jarrette Aycock was Dad's immediate superior in Kansas when he got the call to Africa; later, at the Nazarene college, I tried as editor of the campus newspaper to get Dr. Cantrell and the administration to name the new campus building after him, as he had been chair of the college board when Dad and Mom were students. To no one's surprise, they chose to name it "Jernigan," the new boys' dorm, not "Aycock Hall."

"Gruntbig," the noun my parents invented so that I would never hear and thus never say "shit," was early so fixed in my ear and mouth that it still embarrasses me to say or write it. Most of my other early power words, too, were from a prudish Christian word-list hammered into children to keep them unspotted from the world. The s– trio, "you must be Saved and Sanctified as a Second definite work of grace," the "holiness" preachers thundered.

Getting "saved" and "sanctified" had specific actions and meanings attached: both happened on your two bended knees, buttocks elevated, head down, in front of the whole church, at the altar. Being saved commanded ceasing sinning; being sanctified took out the root of evil. "Amen" and "Hallelujah" ricocheted off the ceiling to welcome the stray sinner to the Nazarene sheepfold.

"Holiness," as an identifying label for the Nazarenes among the fringe groups of Evangelical Christians, linked them with the ultra-fringe Pentecostals. These people were wilder, more ecstatic in worship, than even the Nazarenes. They would hold meetings that would last longer into the night, and they sometimes broke into a sort of gibberish which had to be translated, which they called "speaking in tongues."

Somewhat more dignified, the Nazarene dialect used old pronouns and verbs, "thou, thee, hast, hath"; "whosoever looketh upon a woman to lust after her hath committed adultery with her already in his heart." These hoary sounds from the King James Version of the Bible, our constant study and our preachers' textbook, echoed in our hymns: "How firm a foundation/ Ye saints of the Lord," "What more can he say/ Than to you he hath said?" "Jesus, the very thought of Thee." Our word-hoard was as strange as Hasid Yiddish in Anglo- or French-Outremont, as different as seminary Latin from Cardinal Ouellette's Sunday sermon to the Catholics. "Come ye out from among them, and be ye separate, saith the Lord." "Father, you know Latin," said wry old Earl Crawford, on the front porch of his Island Brook general store, pointing to the posted hours for *les messes* on the Eglise sign across Rte. 212; "what do

A.M. and P.M. stand for?" Clever priest grinned, shot back, "A.M. is avant midi, and P.M. is (a)pres midi."

Some of the degrees earned by my father's saintly teachers and preachers set them off from my own eventual academic badge: my lofty Ph. D., I was told, stood for Piled Higher and Deeper. B. F. Neely had B. O. (Bachelor of Oratory) and was from Hamlin, where Dad went to high school. Dr. Willie Noble King, who taught me koine (kitchen and New Testament) Greek, had an S. T. D. (Doctor of Sacred Theology).

Narcissa, Dad's oldest sibling, was "Aunt Sister" to all us Poteets and Cleggs; the youngest and smallest, Grace, was "Biggie." For that matter, even when I was 6, any preacher was "brother" and the church women who served fried chicken ("dinner on the grounds") after Sunday morning worship were all "sisteren." "Brother Sims remembers you as Jarrette," said Sister Kuykendall at the District Assembly. All believers are family, just as in the human family, red and yellow, black and white, "all have sinned and come short of the glory of God." They must repent and be saved, and then pray for the second definite work of grace, to root out original sin.

Even in the first week of grade eight in Bethany, my parents' college town, after having been springboarded over grade seven because my schooling in Swaziland and South Africa equipped me to leap ahead in the American system, I was so innocent of the exact nuances of some English words that I said "fuck" in class. A shocked silence, but no punishment—after all, I talked funny and wore short brown pants. And got straight "A"s.

My parents' invented word, "gruntbig," was not the only safeguard they put around me to keep my mouth clean. "Nigger" was a word I never heard them say; later, in Africa, I heard "Kaffir" but never said it, nor did I ever spit "Voetsek" ("get out of here") at any person; the Afrikaners used it routinely to discipline blacks. I may have said it to a bad dog, as my December job was selling Christmas cards and calendars in our white suburb,

Nancefield. Dad and Mom came to work with "coloureds," the mixed race people of the Cape Province and Kliptown.

Nazarenes called themselves "holiness people," and they accepted as faith partners the Pilgrim Holiness, Plymouth Brethren, and Wesleyan Methodists. The New Testament's fifth book, Acts, was the scene of the opening moment of this "movement." To begin to spread the gospel (the "god-spell," the message of Christ), the "apostles," a.k.a. "disciples," gathered after the Resurrection in Jerusalem in an "upper room," and the Holy Spirit descended on them; tongues of fire appeared above their heads, and when they emerged onto the balcony before an international, multilingual host of humans, they spoke. and "every man heard them in his own tongue."

But despite the Nazarene self-identification with "holiness" people, they had a kinship with the more radical Pentecostals which they tried to deny. My father gave me a book, with some apprehension, titled *Miracle on Azusa Street*, about the unacknowledged past of the West Coast wing of the Nazarene church. "I give you this little book on the understanding that you never use it against the church," he said. Reading it, I felt a strong kinship with these people in Los Angeles, from whom came one of the first Nazarene "cardinals," or General Superintendents, P.F. Bresee. They had such strong faith that they were unruffled by poverty. No money for food? "God will provide." Dad had lived by this confidence exactly, using the same words (and with the same results—food would show up!) when we were on hard lines in Duncanville, after his missionary work was over and his church at Cedar Hill could not or would not pay his salary, forcing him to move us to a house set up on blocks in a field of mud, and to try and fail at selling encyclopedias, becoming a template clerk at Ling-Temco-Vought (he failed the required course to learn the work), ending as a clerk counting loads at the Dallas garbage dump in West Dallas (he insisted I call it the Department of Sanitation). He came out of this hard time only by taking a teaching job at the Duncanville Elementary School, teaching sixth grade.

My closest pal at Cedar Hill had been Leland Paris, the son of the Pentecostal preacher. Much later, around 2010, I learned that at his death, William Franklin Dallas, mother's father, had been District Superintendent of the Dallas District of the "Pentecostal Church of the Nazarene."

In my formation as a word-person, grade one in Bremersdorp school was taught half in Afrikaans. On the mission station I was picking up Swazi words. At the five-year missionary term's end, in 1952, I was fluent in Afrikaans and Siswati-Zulu: *Onse Vater wat in die hemele ist, Laat Ü naam geheilig word* opened the Lord's Prayer. *Endleleni yonke kungu Jesu/ Umsindisi wame, endleleni yonke...* rang out as our twenty-car motorcade rolled into the mission station on arrival from LaGuardia via Gander, Shannon, Lisbon, Monrovia, Leopoldville, and Johannesburg; the people lining the road and the brick walls were singing "All the way along it is Jesus/ He's our Savior," in Swazi.

Bharati Mjukherjee, novelist, followed her early high-caste Calcutta eduction with the shift to British boarding school when she was eight; when I met her, she was teaching at McGill and spoke fluent French (though at that time, how would I know?). In *Days and Nights in Calcutta*, she writes "When we learn a new language, we bend our personalities."

Aside from the quick lesson about saying "fuck," I first spoke publicly (before a group) in 1953, after our return from South Africa. As Dad traveled about Texas and Oklahoma to raise funds for the mission field, he took me along, and I was asked to talk to a Sunday school class about Africa. Soon I was traveling by myself, by train or bus, up into Kansas, west to Tucson, to talk about the mission field. My little red-vinyl bound note and ledger book, the spine long fragged, outlines my topics on the first page:

WORK IN THREE AREAS. White–Colored–Native.

1. Farm work, hospital-mud brick house. –grass–hills–giant trees, sisala bushes–daggers. Interest in colored. Town–courthouse. Tent revivals.

2. Jo-burg work: Church; school–Melvin Cupido, Sammy Moonsamy, George Taylor, Mr. Birkenstock.

3. White work–Program –Se net n voord vir Jesus.

4. NOW–branching out:—Nyasaland.

Then I began to preach at "Youth Revivals." I had a steel "cut" engraving made to send ahead to put my picture in the local newspaper in Denison, Texas, in Tucson, in Sweetwater, Abilene, Wichita, and Muskogee. Dad bought me my first suit. In my little redbook, it shocks me to read that my Thursday night sermon drove home the "truth" that the fires of hell would burn forever because they were chemical.

Entering Bethany Nazarene College as a religion major, I studied New Testament Greek for two years. To open John, the fourth Gospel, *en arche hay ho logos* ("In the beginning was the Word"), echoes Genesis. I earned a Boy Scout merit badge in language with my Afrikaans, tested by Miss Geraldine Huhnke, German professor (her name means "little hen," but I never blarted it out in her hearing), and I later read *Die Erl-Konig* and Goethe's *Faust* in her classes.

In my one year at Oklahoma University (M.A., 1962), I passed the German graduate reading exam ("Jeez, I thought he was gonna give you the Iron Cross," said Jerry Fiderer, listening by the door as I got the word); I took one semester of University of Arkansas correspondence-course Latin (hence "Razorback Latin," after the football team), and after studying a paperback *Learn French in 30 Days*, passed the French one.

Then it was Minnesota rather than Berkeley because the great university near Peoples' Park required Latin or Greek, and I didn't trust my smattering of either. At Minnesota I already had the two required, so I plunged into Old English. I took a reading course in Middle English poetry with the tall Vermont-born professor ("Yes, I will take you on, though my Old Norse is a bit rusty," Huntington Brown said). I taught undergraduate Chaucer for Spring quarter, 1964 (the new medievalist who had taught me graduate Chaucer in the first quarter having been killed in a car crash driving home to Wisconsin for Christmas).

In Montreal, Marianopolis evening school gave me twelve people with whom to start speaking French, and it did not hurt that the nun who opened the course moved up to become dean at new Dawson College, her place taken by a fetching redhead from Lyon. It took me forty years to begin rattling away publicly in French (*Calisse, apres quarante ans ici, c'est pas un cahot, tabarnouche!*), but I published in *La societe historique acadienne: lescahiers*. And one opening night at the Teatre du Nouveau Monde, I watched, my hair twitching, as the Virgin Mary raised her arms and began to strip in the opening performance of *Les Fees ont Soif*, sending at least a third of the audience charging for the exits, mouths foaming and rosary beads clutched.

Remembering as I heard Nova Scotians speak their classic, older English, in 1972, that Mother had said "If it come a rain," using the old subjunctive, I began to collect the first dictionary of the South Shore; on publication in 1983, *Maclean's* magazine saluted it with a one-page news story: "A Museum of Dead Words." They got it half-right.

In Budapest, traveling to gather avchat words (airplane slang), in five days I learned three words in Hungarian: yes, no, and beer (*sör*). Habla (have) una poquitito espanol (small Spanish) and lch spreche ein bischen schlecht deutsch (less German).

For a few years now, anyone who Googles my name brings up, first off, "My Fake Conversion," a four-page sarcastic nose-thumbing at the Nazarenes who sent me onward with the B.A. in 1961. In the last paragraph, "finger-fucking" earned me a chiding from a friend for its impoliteness. I guess I never learn.

Am I Special or What?

When in 1952, a few months after I, at age twelve, with my family had returned from five years missionary service in Africa, the school system in Texas, testing me in the last few days of the sixth grade, advised my father that I should skip a grade and enter the eighth, he announced the proposal to me by saying that he would permit this boon only if I would promise "never to think that you are better than anyone else."

I am writing now to say that I have tried. But after much time, only recently have I begun to admit to myself that there are a few of us humans around who have more to give than most. And one of us, my own father, was kicked around like any dog by the church, by the economic system, by the new technologies and psychotherapists, and by the big cities, and only his God was faithful to him, allowing him to give as best and as much as he could, to others.

I myself have written and published six books, all dictionaries of slang in different speech communities. All are still in print; one I published myself has now been picked up in revised version for sale across North America. As a lexicographer, I am by some scholar's measure, a practitioner of the fourth most respected profession, after, you know, surgeons and so forth. The one of my books that was selling slowly I remaindered myself. I have taught English literature and language at three universities for thirty-six years. But this self-promotion is making me uneasy. May I reproduce what I wrote about myself in the third person, on the end of my application for early retirement?

Beginning in my deeper exploration of the late Victorian literary and cultural history in which folklore, linguistics, and anthropology first rose, my research has yielded scholarship at the cutting edge of the envelope, useful to such writers as George Elliott Clarke, Governor-General's Award-winning poet, Paul Ledoux, ex-president of the League of Canadian Playwrights, and Robert MacNeil, of *MacNeil-Lehrer Newshour*, actor, broadcaster, and novelist.

Every leave Concordia University has granted me I have repaid in productive publication, save only the first (1973–74) in which I learned some roads not to take, and through a winter's residence in Mexico, became a better teacher. My first book, *The South Shore Phrase Book: A Nova Scotia Dictionary*, was received with more scholarly plaudits than any succeeding book, but each project has been more challenging than the last, and the work on police slang will be the most challenging.

But all of my work bears on, and offers raw material on which to base, ways to understand the response of nineteenth- and twentieth-century human beings to technology, organized sports, and the media. I have regularly written and published essays which show this potential for the products of my research.

Oops! My teacher's eye has just discovered that I gave you a passage not in the third person, but once more in the first! So at the risk of boring repetition, may I reproduce the passage I at first intended to broadcast in this limited fashion? The first was in fact appended to my application for a last sabbatical leave, the last six months before retirement, and, aware that such a boon is not traditional in the academy, I wrote the following to be appended to my plea for early release:

> Those of you who serve on several committees in this university may have noticed that a member of the English department with a name remarkably similar to

mine is applying for a half-year sabbatical leave for the Fall term of 1998.

Though he has not been elected by his departmental colleagues to many powerful committee jobs in his 31-year career with the university, he has always volunteered/or extra duties in thesis reading and tutorial teaching. His research has expanded the envelope of language studies, and has enriched language of the poetry of G.E. Clarke, fiction of Robert MacNeil, and the archive of slang words in several fields where lie the raw evidence of the impact on humans of "machines" in senses both literal (cars, motorcycles, airplanes) and metaphorical (organized sports) since 1800. He has always been a passionate and dedicated teacher, only handicapped in a few of those years by the disappointments of any life in the contemporary maelstrom and the increasing pressures of workload stress in the university. In fact, given his commitment to teaching, he has met the challenge of larger and more classes with grace and enthusiasm. He has always repaid the University's investment in him in the form of sabbatical leave, with productive publication. And he has taken advantage, and much appreciated, tlte longstanding orientation of Sir George Williams University, Loyola College, and Concordia University, by which development of new teaching and research fields has been encouraged, especially toward real education or the real world.

I hope that you will see fit both to grant his leave and give him the boon of early retirement—an experience which John Laffey has described, in perhaps somewhat of an ill temper, as being "unchained from a urinal."

* * *

Am I special? I let you, dear reader, decide. ("You're silly," said Cassie.)

July 29, 1999
Not sure how long it has been since I have written in this document, but it has been a long time. I just read it through. The little list of items put off is interesting because I did them quite handily after writing it. Like Castaneda's persona in *A Yaqui Way of Knowledge*, I seem to be committed somehow to writing before action (analogous to joke first, act after). Anyways, I have completed the projected travels for this summer: I flew on the last of my Aeroplan (Air Canada) points to Vancouver, and sailed for five nights and four days with Gary Geddes, my friend, literary agent, and fellow early retiree from Con U, up the British Columbia coast from Horseshoe Bay to Powell River; I took the bus and ferries back, for two days in Vancouver, with Eric and Helen Jeanes in West Vancouver in their magnificent house with its beach and view of the city and whole harbour, then with Victor Janoff, my ex-student, gay journalist, M.A. candidate in criminology with project on violence against gays, recovering sex, drug, drink, tobaccoholic, near Commercial and Broadway, in a part of the city where people more on the edge than Eric and Helen live. I returned with my head full of images of the coast and inlets, with a list of books Gary prescribed, and much inspiration from his energy in carrying on with teaching and writing after the hiatus with Con U. After two days of being at home, I drove with Cassie and Alvie the Westie dog to Niagara, where we participated in a 50th wedding anniversary celebration with her relatives. On return, I had a few more days to prepare for an overnight trip with Martin Stone to Kingston to see my surrogate son, Chris Coyle, married, an event at which, to my surprise, I had forgotten Morgan, my younger son, his lady Cathy, and their daughter Kailan were present, delightfully. There were also many members of Aaron and Morgan's old hockey buddies,

from Westmount. In between all this I read *The Poisonwood Bible*, so apropos of my own African experience and attitude to the missionary (crazy) impulse and effort.

I also, along the way, wrote out a page of items to enter in this writing, under the heading "I will (to) write a memory of perception of Africa every day. Try after breakfast. If nothing comes, set a later time to do it. Usw. Needless to say, I have not done this. But it is amazing how many separate memory tags turned up in my handwritten list...

- Melvin Cupido Sammy Moonsamy
- Durban—"alone with Jesus," the beach, the jellyfish
- Tucks Farm
- Boksburg, Uncle and Auntie Jenkins, the cadet unit and uniform
- Acornhoek, the pineapple field in front of the house, the threat of boarding school The circus in Nancefield, the bioscope in Kliptown ("Two-Gun Tex" and "Pistol Pete"), the girlfriend from school and the kiss between the post office (separate entrances for "European" and "Non-european") and home
- Albertus and Ethel Pop
- "I won't go back until Nelson Mandela is President"
- The parking ticket in Joburg resulting from my misreading the sign, with collection notice (summons?) delivered by a policeman to Nancefield

Come See

"Come see the American preacher who can jump ten feet high!" the poster in the post office said. Staring, I read "Wednesday to Sunday," then, at the bottom, "Revival in the Tent on Boundary Road" … "KLIPTOWN NAZARENE CHUIRCH." So this, this green tent, these people, is to reach new seekers so that Dad and Reverend Chalfant can start the church.

Not like church, this. A big tent in the field beside the first, main street over in the township. I remember it was a littler tent, in Swaziland, when Dad took me and the Swazi translator Dhlamini in that big Jeep out into the bush, and we put up a tent in a clearing near a river, for a revival. But here it's the houses and stores of Kliptown is on one side, and Nancefield on the other, lots of people living close together, and those stubbly gray walls and columns on the front of the stores. Regular church is mostly on Sundays, everywhere I've been. Now, on Wednesday, in this tent, with the light from the paraffin lanterns, we sit on folding chairs on the bare grass floor, not on hard benches on concrete, indoors. Noisy, the people talking, mother playing "Revive Us Again" on the pedal organ.

Dad and Reverend Chalfant are at the end, on a platform. The preacher who can jump must be him, because he is big and tall, not like Dad. Healthy and wiry and always moving, Dad can ride a horse, which is how he and Uncle Jim did their traplines in West Texas before Dad went to Bethany to college. But the jumping preacher is about half again as wide as Dad is, and taller. He told me he had been a basketball player at his Nazarene college.

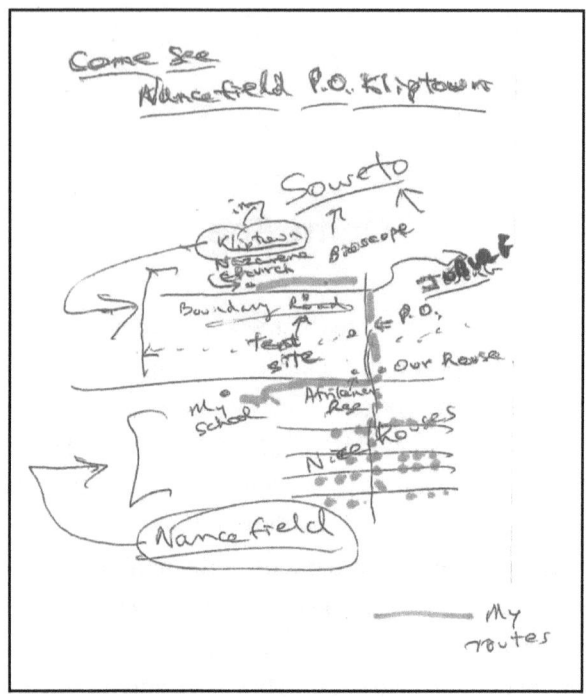

Author's hand-drawn map of Nancefield

At regular church, I sit with Mother, Steve, and baby Jim. Here I'm beside Melvin, who I met yesterday, and his friends Sammy and John. Wait, they are starting the service. Dad is saying "Come to the Lord, all ye that labour." It is windy out, and the tent flaps and the lanterns sway. I sure hope and pray the ropes hold, but for now Dad looks happy and excited and hopeful.

What a night that was! A lot of people were lekker, I mean eager, to join these Nazarenes. Why, ik ken nie, except we are laughing and serious both. They were so caught up in the music of the meeting that they did not notice at first (I did) when the tent broke loose at one end. But when the lanterns crashed and broke, everybody ran out. And everybody got out okay.

So it did start the church, because the men helping Dad pass concrete blocks down the row right now, George Taylor and Albertus Pop, and Mr. Vanzeeberg, they were saved at the tent revival meeting. And now, just in this one morning, the back wall of the new church is four rows high. I am giving out paper cups of water. And Mother and Mrs. Cupido (Melvin's Mom) and Audrey Vanzeeberg (new Nazarenes) are getting soup and sandwiches ready. Mrs. Cupido is thin and looks old, and Audrey is young and beautiful, but they call each other "sister," since they got saved.

It's hot in the sun, here just down the road from where the tent stood and then blew down. And further along dusty Boundary Road, almost to the post office road up to our house in Nancefield, is the bioscope, where Dad preached every Sunday afternoon after the revival. "The Grand," the sign says in big letters, and "American Movies," in little ones.

My father, Henry T. Poteet, born March 3, 1911, County Line, Fisher County, West Texas. Coyote trapper; B.A., Bethany-Peniel College; Nazarene pastor, Oklahoma, Kanas, 1938–45; Nazarene missionary to Africa, 1946–52; pastor, Texas, 1952–56; counsellor, Texas, 1956–61. Died 2003, Austin, TX.

So fast, all this. My school in Nancefield is solid brick, like our house-red, not gray like these concrete blocks. Mr. Potgieter has all the grades in one room, from the little kids to my Form Four and the older ones. Mr. Potgieter is taller than Mr. Wust was, and he talks more softly. And at recess, we line up outside to get soup, and then can run down to the gates or play marbles.

I must be dozing off. Dad is sweating now, but he is smiling. Mother has laid the sandwiches out on the plank table by the road. I'm hungry.

A Small Breach in Apartheid in Nancefield, P.O. Kliptown, in 1949

Red and yellow
Black and white
They are precious in His sight.
Jesus loves the little children of the world.

At ten years old, I had seen a cow spurt blood and die—knife across the massive throat—during a school field trip to a slaughterhouse. But I had never before seen a human being come within inches of being crushed until the five-year old neighbor girl from across the street tumbled away from the spinning rear wheel of her brother's car, in front of me and the twenty coloured Nazarenes, my father's new converts, suddenly turning to watch because the car threw gravel as he twisted the wheel and roared away into the white township where we lived. We were in my family's back yard in Nancefield, P. O., Kliptown, in 1950. I never knew their family name, but their house was older than ours, a gabled, white stucco, typical Afrikaner two-story house. We were standing, talking, in the afternoon sunshine, having ice tea and cookies. And the sudden anger that moved the Afrikaans young man to act out and then light out was caused, innocently, by my father.

In 1948 Dad had been directed by the Nazarene mission council on the South African field to establish work among the "coloured" people in the townships just southwest of Johannesburg. He and Morris Chalfant, a bluff, burly American from Chicago, erected a tent in Kliptown, and held a weeklong set of services. The posters advertising the tent revival invited people to "Come see the American preacher who can jump ten feet high!" (Morris Chalfant, I learned in 2012, had been an ace basketball player at Olivet Nazarene College in Kankakee, Illinois.) There was then as yet no electricity in Kliptown, and so the tent was lit by kerosene lanterns hanging from the interior support poles. On the fourth night, in a windstorm, full of singing people, it blew down. I will never forget the breaking glass and screaming people. But no one, miraculously, was hurt, and Dad rented a movie theatre (the Grand, called, quaintly, a "bioscope") for Sunday afternoon meetings, and then built a cement block church.

The mission board had rented for my family a fine house adjacent to Kliptown, just beyond the post office that served both Nancefield, our spacious "white" town, and teeming Kliptown. Hence our address: "Nancefield, P.O. Kliptown." The post office had two entrances, one for "non-Europeans" and the other, which I as a nine year old used to pick up our mail as I walked back from school, was for "Europeans." (But in apartheid's odd ethnic geography "European" included Chinese; Indians were "non-.) Our house had parquet floors, except for the red-tiled kitchen, a fenced yard, and an apple orchard.

After the church was a reality, with a congregation of at least several score of people, Dad decided to have a picnic at our house and invite his flock. They were mostly "coloureds," mixed-race people with varying skin hues of brown, not black or "white." Many were teachers or secretaries, no miners I am sure. Also in our church were several Indian South Africans-like the coloureds, better educated than tribal black people from the bush, and not so poor.

So they came for the picnic, to our house with its big backyard, on that sunny summer day: George Taylor, who later became a sort of Nazarene bishop, a "district superintendent." Albertus Pop, a public school principal in the coloured section, and his wife, who played piano. My friends, Sammy Moonsamy, later a pastor in the San Francisco area in California, and his and my best friend Melvin Cupido. Melvin's "mother," "Mrs. Cupido," as we always called her, cleaned our house, and I was told, erroneously, that this very old, gaunt, seemingly Indian woman was actually his grandmother, her scapegrace runaway daughter having left her with Melvin to raise, so she could scarper back to Durban, on the Indian Ocean. Audrey Vanzeeberg, a singer, who ended with a career in Houston.

Our house was almost alone at the first corner leading into Nancefield, but across the street the Afrikaner family lived in the only other building between most of Nancefield and the post office, and Kliptown, beyond.

I was in the yard, enjoying the company of the happy people, the warm sunshine, and the Nazarene refreshments, when it happened. The Afrikaner son from across the street was backing his car out, engine roaring and drive wheels whirling. I saw her: he almost ran over his little sister. She tumbled over almost under the right rear wheel. But amazingly, she was not hurt!

Shocked into silence, we all filed into the house. Mother played the piano. And in a few minutes, the mother from across the street came over, sat, and listened to us, cradling her little daughter in her lap.

By the rules set forth for apartheid by laws passed in 1948, any nonwhite person in Nancefield had to have a pass. Mrs. Cupido did not attract anger, for Afrikaners were used to having cleaning ladies (and garden boys) of the proper colour. But a gathering, even a nonpolitical one, was illegal. That being said, it was not the law but the unprecedented sight of so many strange brown faces, relaxing and enjoying themselves across the street from his house, that made the boy boil over.

It makes a balance: a young man angrily, impulsively expresses the unease of his people at the sudden nonwhite gathering in a white town; his mother silently acknowledges that we are all human beings in a turbulent world.

Dad probably knew as little as I did about the new laws, and a church picnic at his own house was a signal gesture of his inner ease, free from any racist twinges at all, with his new friends. In 2012, some older members of Dad's old church remembered that the next pastor, also a white missionary, never allowed any nonwhite person into his house. However, to be free of racist hatred would set any white at odds with Afrikaner neighbours. While we were in Nancefield, my friend Ann Ramsay was on her father's sheep farm in Matathiele, below Pietermaritzburg and northwest toward the mountains from East London; he moved his family to Canada after a couple of years because the mail was being opened, his neighbours resented his not having guns or vicious dogs to control the blacks, and he did not object to black wanderers crossing his land.

With our church picnic Dad actually inadvertently bent our corner of that world away from apartheid, and the event offered a forecast in small of what was eventually to come for the whole country, after some violence and many years—the end of the Boer regime—and as well a main means by which it would come. An Afrikaner might well fear the British and American religious appeal to the oppressed peoples of the land. Nelson Mandela was a Methodist. Desmond Tutu was an Anglican. Missions and churches brought black, coloured, and Indian peoples together. It was in Kliptown, in 1955, that a huge illegal meeting of the African National Congress members and supporters drafted the Charter of Freedom (their "Declaration of Independence," according to Nelson Mandela), encircled by police small vans known as "scorpions," for their short whip antennas. In the dispersal of the crowd, Mandela dressed as a milkman to escape without being arrested.

When I returned to see the changes in early December of 2012, Melvin Cupido drove me past the place where our house had been, and both there and on the main road through Kliptown no trace remains of our house, Melvin and Mr. Pop's school, or the Grand movie theatre. It is all uniform, neat, smallish housing now, and so as apartheid took force, the comfortable Nancefield whites must have had to move, just as blacks, coloureds, and Indians had been forcibly displaced from their neighbourhoods.

Nelson and Winnie Mandela had to watch their home in Sophiatown, a residential nonwhite suburb closer to the city which Mandela describes as nearly a cultural centre, like Soho in England, to their famous address, now a museum, in Kliptown (now known as the Eldorado section of Soweto).

I never knew the name of our young impetuous Afrikaner neighbour. In fact, I knew almost no Afrikaners in the years in Swaziland and the Transvaal, save only my two teachers in the two schools for whites I attended. In Bremersdorp it was Mr. Wust, short and stout, and a kind and merciful person. He had a rule that he would administer one stroke of the cane for each arithmetic problem done incorrectly. But when on the first test, I missed thirty, he looked at the paper, shook his head, and said, "I cannot do this," and let me offer, as we say in Quebec. It was only the first grade!

And the last three years, in Nancefield, I remember my teacher, Mr. Johannes Stephanus duPrees Potgieter, as of average build, tall, always sitting straight in his chair behind his desk, calm, well organized, and clear in all his explanations. His first surname, "duPrees," likely his mother's name, is of French Huguenot origin. Thus it is my own direct evidence of the odd congruence in South African history of the sizable, dominant white people of Dutch Reformed extraction, and a smaller but noticeable population of Protestant refugees from the prevailing Catholic regime in France. These two displaced peoples intermarried, and both were more easily comfortable with each other than with the only other "white" group, the British. They were "Boers" (farmers) and cultivators of vineyards rather than resource-extraction colonizers, like Cecil Rhodes and others following the discovery of diamonds in 1870 in Kimberley and gold in 1886 in Witwatersrand (Johannesburg). Believing that their God had given them the land in which to be fruitful and multiply, they felt mandated to use the black natives as pack animals and breeders, and to treat them with disciplinary measures if they opposed the will of Jehovah. The Dutch and the French were there to stay. The Brits, conversely, were seen as temporary opportunists, there to get the gold, platinum, and diamonds, and run with the money. In fact, a surprising number of the British people I met in Montreal had tried South Africa for a couple of years, and then decamped for Canada (Alan Rose of the Canadian Jewish Congress; my friend Ann Ramsay Payson's bagpiper father Gordon Ramsay; Alexander Niven, pressman extraordinaire and union leader, of Port Elizabeth and the *Montreal Star*). Returning to the bare shelves of post-World War II England was not an attractive option. I call it a new version of the old three-cornered trade route, after the old Nova Scotia-Caribbean-Mother England triangle for rum, trees, and ships. If you recall Charlotte Bronte's *Jane Eyre*, or read between the lines in Jane Austen's *Mansfield Park*, you may see that it was not only Dutch men who found dark female skin fetching.

Moreover, Potgieter is a common surname around Port Elizabeth, East London, and Grahamstown, in the East Cape. In my hotel in Port Elizabeth in November 2012, the oil paintings in the *frühstuck kamer* (breakfast room) off the lobby were by a Potgieter. Athol Fugard, the Nobel Prize nominee playwright who wrote and staged clandestine anti-apartheid basement plays in the 1970s, was on his mother's side a Potgieter. I noticed this fact about him with a start when I came upon it in a book in Maurice Podbrey's condo in Cape Town, early in November 2012, at the beginning of my return trip to research this project. For it was Maurice Podbrey who helped me bring Fugard to my university a score of years before I retired, when Fugard, already under suspicion by the Boer government, came to Montreal to direct a play at Maurice's theatre. When I introduced the dissident playwright to a room full of mixed black and white people, united by our ties to the country still in struggle, the feeling in the room was almost palpably an air of tangible fear, exactly what the air carried in South Africa after 1948. I remembered that feeling, and later asked Frank Chalk, my coach in South African history, who was also in that room, whether he noticed it. He said emphatically that he did. And at the party after the event, from my house, Fugard's daughter disappeared to go dancing in Montreal with a black youth she had just met, an adventure she even then could not do at home.

It may seem odd that I would know only these two men, Mr. Wust and Mr. Potgieter, from the Afrikaner people, since in my years there, they were not only the most numerous of our fellow whites, but also the voting majority that elected in 1948 the Nationalist government. I did not know it then, but that new government, elected under the banner "die wit man moet altyd baas wees" ("the white man must always be boss"), passed the racist, inflammatory apartheid laws that would make the country for the next fifty years a seething pot of protest, mostly nonviolent, and recriminatory murderous repressive reprisal.

But you must understand that in those early years I was in a Nazarene missionary cocoon. My world in Bremersdorp was the road from the farm, at least a mile long, which I traveled daily on my small Raleigh bicycle to get to school. I would reach the mission gates, just past the church I attended every Sunday, and take the bus to my school, and return the same way at day's end.

In Nancefield, my perimeter was, from our house, the road past the post office to East (now Boundary) Road, the route to the church Dad built about a half mile to the left from the corner. The only other road I walked was straight from the front of our house to the Nancefield school for white students, where Mr. Potgieter taught me. We were given hot soup from large barrel-vats outdoors at recess, and if we liked, could play marbles the rest of the break (I was no good at marbles), or buy tiny cans of sweetened condensed milk from a small van at the school gate (I loved it).

As for Johannesburg, the enormous city at the center of the urban area of the Rand (the strip east and west where gold was mined, marked by huge yellow dunes made up of the dumped slag—excavated, waste underground soil). I almost never saw the central city. I remember the slag heaps, striking and clearly man-made, beside the highway we would use to go to other townships for church, like Protea, where Morris Chalfant had built his church for the coloureds, and another with the unforgettable name "White City New Jabavu." Dad did one time drive me in to the belly of the beast to take me to the American library. It was a memorable break in routine, because he checked out a book which was the only non-Nazarene book I read in the five years there (I was, as you may guess, an avid, voracious reader). Written by a Pacific theatre World War II chaplain, it was titled *Praise the Lord and Pass the Ammunition*. So I suppose its author, a fellow minister, could be trusted not to corrupt my young mind. Dad did not know that in a solitary exploration in the Bremersdorp school library, I had found a book that described the ride made by Lady Godiva, in legendary British history, and I knew enough even in grade three not to ask anyone anything about this curiously fascinating tale (well, okay, image).

The other result of that motor trip into Johburg was that Dad had asked me to translate a parking regulation sign that was in Afrikaans, and though I could rattle away in that language (as I could then in Swazi, too), I got the rule exactly wrong. Two weeks later, a policeman from the city rode up to our house in Nancefield to deliver a citation for the infraction. The fine must not have been much, as Dad did not strap me for the offence.

On my return trip to do the follow-up part of this project, just completed in this last month of 2012, I met a number of

Afrikaners, mostly on corners, on buses, or in stores, and I spoke with them only in English, my early Afrikaans skills having been overlaid by two years of college German and three trips to Berlin and Bochum, Germany.

The one person I met on this return trip who might, I thought at first, have been Afrikaans in origin, was so immediately, unexpectedly helpful in feeding me information and reading for my project that I did not think to ask, until after I returned, his exact place in the white spectrum of the country. Jonathan Pons, now an opthalmologist in Swaziland, was South African born and educated, operating an eye clinic at a Catholic hospital in Siteki, in the eastern highland near the Mozambique border. His wife, Helen, inherited a farm with a grand manor house from her grandfather, a Johannesburg lawyer, and they had created a B & B where I spent a weekend. I swam in their pool, had tea at their tiny Sunday afternoon prayer meeting, and profitably used a whole day of bad weather devouring the first third of Michael Cassidy's *The Passing Summer*. a key last-minute cram-feast to acquaint me with the place of the church (in this case the Anglican) in the front lines of the anti-apartheid struggle. Rev. Cassidy, educated at private school in Durban (as was Dr. Jonathan Pons), went on to Cambridge and California's Fuller Theological Seminar, attended the first prayer breakfast (Billy Graham, for JFK), and returned to his homeland to be present at virtually every bloody riot-repression over many years until the Afrikaners gave up.

Dr. Pons got my attention by telling me, in one word, "bosberaad," how the Nationalist government was persuaded to free Nelson Mandela and make way for the decisive election that made him president. In Mandela's autobiography, *Long Walk to Freedom*, he gives no details but emphasizes how secret the negotiations had to be, since many African National Congress supporters could not see any reason to meet with the hated, murderous, wily enemy face to face, and talk.

The crucial secret meeting was called a bosberaad. Though the word is Afrikaans, its importance is signaled by its appearing in not only English but also Dutch, Spanish, and German, in today's word-lists. A "raad" is a council or discussion, a word related to the more familiar cousin word, "rat" as in "rathaus," German for "city council house" or "town hall." "Bos" means "woods" or "bush," in its English form "bask" since 1297, according to the *Oxford English Dictionary*. "Bosquet," in French, is a grove or shrubbery. Hence the county south of Dallas where my grandfather (Lewis, or Louis) cut wood for a dollar a day when he was 17 was Bosque ("Bosky") County, a trace of the French Voyageur track from Quebec toward New Orleans and Beaumont, Texas. In the *Collins English Dictionary*, "bosberaad" is defined as "from Afrikaans, a meeting in an isolated venue to break a political deadlock."

The euphemistic, shadowy identification of the source in the Collins English word-book is in a curious way fitting. For I have so far not found in print any exact description of the event or the venue. It does not figure at all in the rather dark account that is Michael Cassidy's *The Passing Summer*. After all, the book was published in 1989, the darkest, bloody time just before what one South African columnist recently called "the Dawn of Freedom," when Mandela was freed a year later. But Dr. Pons, perhaps because he is a friend of Rev. Cassidy, said that the secret meeting was in an actual woods, between men only, from every faction in the bloody struggle, who stared each other straight and steadily in the eyes, and talked until it was worked out—that was the "bosberaad." We may guess that the Afrikaners, already having moved Mandela to a less severe prison in Cape Town but still funding Zulu men secretly to kill other blacks (to show that a change would be more of a bloodbath), eventually believed what their foes were saying, that the bloodbath would continue until every South African had a vote, the ANC was unbanned, and Mandela was freed. The shadows that still surround the event may have to do with its initial secrecy, but it perhaps also reflects the political incorrectness of the meeting itself. (OK, feminists, how did brave Winnie Mandela fare in the struggle, pure of heart and courageous as she was? She certainly supported her husband through the years of his imprisonment, but she did not become "mother" of her country.)

I returned from my trip without being sure of the provenance of Dr. Pons' surname. It is indeed a rare puzzle, but a Google search before dawn one morning gave me the name of the Durban Anglican school where he played rugby, and I Skyped a call to him so we could laugh together about my mistake. Pons is indeed from French, and so not all of the Huguenots became Boers.

I have only one other sharp memory of any contact with the Afrikaner people. One day as I walked up the short part of the road between the post office and my home, I was hand in hand with a girl from school, whose name I do not remember but who was certainly, with her dark eyes and black hair, a daughter of Afrikaans parents. We kissed goodbye, for good as it turned out, because Mrs. Cupido, my friend Melvin's adopted mother, cleaning our house, saw the kiss and told my father. He gave me the strap, as he did only for signs of any budding sexual interest or even curiosity. Spare the rod, yes, in this case the leather belt, but he later volunteered that his theory of child-rearing was in this aspect less than perfect. I of course have always blamed his strap for my having remained a virgin to the age of 22, and the cause of any number of sexual improprieties in my behavior since that time. Offhand I cannot think of any, but there must have been a few, and I want to get as much fun as I can out of that Nazarene prudery and my consequent pain.

And I know by heart, and can sing, the first verse and chorus of the most popular love song from the Afrikaans republic, its title the name, I'm sure, of my sweet, cute, innocent little female friend:

Mijn Sarie Marais ist zo ver von mijn hart,
Ik wees nie wat om te doen.
Sy het dan die wyk von die Mooi rivier gewoon
Want daar woon mijn Sarie Marais.

(My Sara Marsh is so far from my heart,
I know not what I'm to do.
She did near the bend of the Mooi River live
For there lives my Sara Marie.)

And the chorus:

O bring mij terug na die ou Transvaal,
Daar war mijn Sarie woon,
Daronder in die mealies by die ou dooringboom,
Want daar woon mijn Sarie Marais.

(O bring me back to the old Transvaal,
There where my Sarie lives
Down yonder in the cornfield by the old thorn tree,
For there lives my Sara Marsh Marie.)

The recurrent theme of Michael Cassidy's book is that it is only love that can heal thwe worst divisions and separations, hatreds, and apartnesses. How could the non-fucking Nazarenes get it so upside down? How could the Boers, ditto? Only in a world without any kind of a *god*. Only poor wrongheaded humans fuck up so badly.

- Selling calendars and Christmas cards door to door
- Parents' return to Africa and tour in 1978
- Athol Fugard
- Dates of travel—ask Dad—immediately he came up with

our departure from Durban, very near March 3, 1952
- School-sweetened condensed milk, soup, marbles, Mr. Potgieter
- Learning to cook (at least cakes) when Mother was in hospital having Dewey. Table Mountain
- First African school in Bremersdorp—missing 30 arithmetic problems—the forgiven 30 strokes of the whip
- The green mamba snake, my bicycle, Mrs. Hynd, my dog
- Train trip Elizabethville to Joburg—Dad's "certificate" signed by FDR, for raising money for war bonds
- George Taylor
- Mr. Birkenstock

While in Niagara, I discovered that one of Cassie's aunts, Joy, and her husband Ralph Pettibone, live in Red Deer, Alberta, where there was a Nazarene College when I was at Bethany. And from talking with them, I learned that it is long gone, and that Red Deer Press is totally independent. I of course had visions of approaching them with this manuscript…

August 4, 1999
Returning to the writing, with some corrections and material resulting from conversations with Dad, who is now 88 years old, and though be claims Mother's memory is better, has sharp recollections when I ask questions, and much more than I ask. The group of missionaries among whom we were one family, which I remembered as numbering forty, was actually only thirteen in our group, another group of nine to follow in a week. So the total was twenty-one; and when we were flying from Leopoldville to Elizabethville, on the charter airplane, we took on two Jehovah's Witness missionaries to make up a full airplane. Among the group were a number of people who were to become close friends of my parents, and whose children in some cases became my friends. They included Elmer Schmelzenbach, whose father

had pioneered Nazarene missions in South Africa, especially Swaziland, during the 1930s, and whose son Harmon was to become a pal of mine and later a third-generation missionary from his family. There were also Bob and Leila Jackson, and a close friend of Dad's with surely the most appropriate surname for his work, Wesley Meek.

In establishing the exact date of our departure, so far as possible from this remove in time, Dad's research turned up the fact that we were, in mid-trip, for three days, in Leopoldville, October 15, 16, and 17 of 1946. We stayed at the ABC Hotel. Dad remembers Wesley Meek's wonderment at a native man he saw while out walking in the city, whose feet "stuck out as far back as forward."

Again, on the date: I tried to establish where we spent nights. Dad remembers no overnight stops until Dakar, North Africa, and then again at Camp Roberts, Monrovia, Liberia. In one of these places, Leila Jackson was diagnosed as having mumps, surely quite serious for an adult; and she did not reveal her condition until we reached the mission station in Swaziland, for fear, obviously, of not being admitted to the various countries through which we passed.

We were passing on a very slow train, pulled by a steam engine, coal-burning, and as it was so hot that windows had to be open, I have clear memories of the cinders blowing in and faces covered with soot. The train was so slow that when once my little hat blew off, Wesley Meek ran out of the compartment, jumped off the train, retrieved it, and caught up to the train to restore the hat to me. I have no memory of this event.

I think it will elucidate the narrative at this point to include an essay I wrote some time ago about my father and the genesis of his project, "Faith of my Father: Sacrifice!" (pronounced as if in French: "sacri–feece").

Faith of My Father: "Sacrifice!"

My father, Henry Theodore Poteet, found his religious faith when he was thirteen, in 1924, at a fundamentalist revival meeting conducted by a circuit-riding preacher, at the open-sided tabernacle in the (Fisher) County Line community on the flat middle plains of West Texas where his father and mother were homesteaders. When this event happened, only forty years had passed since Billy the Kid was killed a few hundred miles west in New Mexico, and only a few years since Pancho Villa was stirring up revolucion in Texas-Mexico border towns not far to the south. The revival where my father found his faith was conducted by Uncle Buddy Robinson, an amazing man who stuttered in ordinary conversation but preached without a stutter, with great fluency, passion, tears, and rhetoric. I heard his voice once on an old phonograph record.

For a lonely boy in that land of sod busters and traplines, "getting right with God" must have been a big event. He was a slender, five-foot-nine farm boy, youngest boy of five sons and caught in the middle of the five girls, and he was lonely, despite all those brothers and sisters. For, you see, most of the memories he has recounted for me of those days are of his solitary, agonized praying in the canyons. Of course he fell to reading and rereading the Bible, and he read in the Old Testament, and heard in the sermons of the preachers, about "sacrifice." God required it: in my own old sermon notes, from my boy preacher days, I typed it in red, one of my texts—Hebrews 9:22—"Without shedding of blood is no remission of sins." But he couldn't, at first, figure out bow he should do it. As a passionate, new Christian, he felt an obligation to obey God, to show his faith, and he thought he had to offer a sacrifice himself! The only animal he could think of—probably the only one over which he had the right—was his dog. And he actually considered doing it! Sacrificing his dog! The Old Testament went into full detail on technique: the knife, the fire, the altar. It's a good thing he kept on reading into the New Testament. His dog was spared, but only by his coming upon the story of Christ, the perfect sacrifice, whose crucifixion wiped out the need for the old sacrifice of the Israelites. It's all in my old sermon notes, again: *"For if the blood of bulls and of goals, and the ashes of an heifer sprinkling the unclean, sanctifieth to the purifying of the flesh: How much more shall the blood of Christ, who through the eternal Spirit offered himself without spot to God, urge your conscience from dead works to serve the living God?"*

So it was that the sacrifice of Christ became the central figure in my father's adolescent imagination, the subject of his mectitations, tears, and prayers in the canyons, and when in 1933 or '34, he decided to leave home to go to college, he decided to study to be a preacher. He saved as much money as he could from his trapping, sold his trapline to his older brother Jim, who went on in his turn to spend his life as a government coyote trapper in and around Midland, West Texas, and Dad went to Bethany Peniel College, a "holiness" institution of "higher learning" in Bethany, Oklahoma. The little town was just about as far outside Oklahoma City as Bethany, in the Bible, had been outside Jerusalem.

When I consider that I've set out to tell in a few pages the story of the faith of this man, who spent his life as a preacher, missionary, and counselor, I am surprised at my own audacity: his faith ruled his whole life and mind. Moreover, it was a particularly intangible, inner faith, not without trouble and questioning, and it played out its immaterial dream in a very material world, through which he walked without fully believing, I think, in its substantial reality. But I am going to try, anyway, and perhaps I can best approach it by sticking to the idea of sacrifice which had so seized him at age thirteen.

He took a degree in history, married, fathered two boys, and served for short periods as preacher to two little Nazarene churches in Western Oklahoma. When the Second World War came, it found him at the church in Manhattan, Kansas, near the huge Topeka air base. He does not seem to have been infected with the war fever which led many American boys to sacrifice themselves for country: he was thirty-one, and twice a father. He became a chaplain at the base, and spent the war Stateside. But shortly after the war ended, he acted on a dream of self-sacrifice more his own, more directly religious, perhaps engendered by the doughboys dying overseas—he volunteered for the mission field. That is, he actually dreamed that throngs of Africans beckoned him and called "Come over and help us." So he, my mother, my brother Steve and I, were on the first plane-load of Nazarene missionaries out of New York's LaGuardia airport after the war, in 1946, bound for Swaziland, South Africa.

I must add one more bit of family history to add depth to the story of the dream, for as 1 have described it so far, the "call to Africa," however romantic, may sound more impulsive than it actually was. As he grew up, my father asked his parents why they had named him "Henry," a name he did not particularly like (the brothers teased him with "Henny"). The other boys received regular he-man names like George, John, Bill, and Jim. "Your father had a boy named Henry, before he came to Texas," they said, "and he died young." Dad later told me that he assumed that be himself, in turn, would die young. But there was a further mystery about the first Henry: his mother was a maid or a servant in the house, and she was either black or, according to Aunt Narcissa, our family historian, Cajun. So Dad's amazing dream came out of this context in which his sense of destiny was born.

His five years as a missionary were not without successes, even triumphs. He built a plain cement-block church himself, working with the men of the new congregation in Kliptown, near Johannesburg; he was one of the first Nazarenes to start work among the "coloureds," the three million métis, or mixed-race people, in South Africa, that tragic land built on injustice and suffering. I have often thought how perfectly right it was that he should have chosen to do his best work there among these people, who were brilliant misfits, outcasts from both white and black, lost in the shadows of apartheid. For he himself didn't exactly fit in. His dream had been fairly unspecific, and the mission council, needing a practical task for every hand, set him at first, to his great disgust, in charge of the mission farm. After all, they said, he had been a farmer in Texas. And as an American, he didn't get along well with some of the British missionaries. In fact, in his perhaps willful ignoring of mission politics, be dared to criticize the prominent British doctor, David Hynd, OBE, CBE, who was head of the huge mission hospital at Bremersdorp, centre of the Nazarene operation, for his practice of sending black patients to the subordinate American doctor, and keeping the white patients for himself. My father was tactless and unpolished beside the smooth Brits. And so it was that, when in the midst of his first furlough, the sabbatical year home after the first term of mission service, the assembled missionaries had to vote on his return to the field, my father lost the vote by the largest majority ever recorded.

It was a terrific blow. The furlough was always a time of high enjoyment. You were home, having given all to follow the call, to risk your life on heathen (possibly cannibal?) shores, you were triumphantly reunited with relatives; and the year's work was to travel around in great honor and celebration all over the States, telling Nazarenes about exotic Africa and the blessed rescue of heathen souls from superstition and darkness. I even got into the act myself, giving talks to the kids in Sunday School and liking it so much that eventually I accepted invitations to travel around the Southwest as a boy preacher. So when, in the middle of the year, the telegram with the bad news caught up with us in California, Dad's tour of triumph was abruptly canceled, and we went back to Bethany, even we boys (four of us by this time) knew that something terrible had happened. Dad went to Kansas City mission headquarters to appeal for an explanation or reversal of the decision; then, when he came back, went straight into the vacant end room of our house, and didn't come out for thirty days. He fasted the whole time. I knew what he was doing: crying and praying, praying and crying, asking God for the explanation he could accept as he could not the mission board's "policy" decision which so contradicted his dream.

I guess it was about that time that I decided Dad had made himself the sacrifice.

For one thing, I learned that the mission board had offered to send him to British Honduras, and he had refused. God only knows what joys or sorrows, maybe even genuine sacrifice, may have awaited us if he had spent the rest of his life in that country, and I had finished growing up there, in Spanish and Creole, watching another of our suffering world's vicious repressions flower into the Sandinista revolution in nearby Nicaragua. He seemed not to know what to do with any passion or purpose for some time after that Christmas 1953. We moved to Duncan, Oklahoma, for a month, where he did some carpentry work. When a church was offered to him in Grand Saline, Texas, he took it, and after a year he lost another vote and had to move on again. The next church didn't vote him out, but it lost so many members, or had so few and so poor, that it could not pay him. When the salary owed reached $800, and an appeal by Brother Garrett, the well-fed, well-dressed, Buick-driving district superintendent, produced no results (I remember the embarrassed silence as he stood, red-faced before us, the church members offereding neither money nor pledges), Dad moved us out and into a frame house just set up on a vacant lot, still up on the blocks, provided rent-free by a friend.

What followed was a succession of failures. He tried to sell vacuum cleaners, sold only one, and for that one had to take an old typewriter in trade in lieu of the down payment, which was to have been his commission. He was hired as a trainee by Ling Temco Vought, the big aircraft manufacturer (later into spacecraft, now defunct) in nearby Grand Prairie, to see if he could learn the work of the template shop, but failed the training course. He even worked a short time as a cabbie in Dallas, and then as a clerk at a garbage dump, recording loads, but his pride wouldn't let him stay. One of my own most painful memories is having half-cruelly mocked him by insisting on calling it the "garbage" department. He preferred "sanitation department."

When he heard that the local elementary school needed a sixth-grade teacher, he went in, got the job, and from then on his life was a happier and more successful one. He did graduate work in counseling, and finished his working life as a dedicated advocate of the Chicano students in a hostile school system near Corpus Christi, and doing fill-in preaching and lots of church counseling. He is still a fairly small man, "*un homme petit*," but he looks more striking than ever, with a white mustache and lines of concern that, when he prays before the congregation with eyes closed and hands upraised, make him look like a prophet. He sacrifices (that word again!) his peace of mind by service as counselor to people in trouble, "bearing," as the Bible enjoins, "their burdens, and so fulfill[ing] the law of Christ." He has finally convinced me that he accepts all that has happened to him in his life, and thanks his God for it all—the aborted missionary career, my brother Steve's death on a motorcycle at age twenty-three, all the pain and change and trouble.

I guess his faith saved him—certainly it did—but when I come to try to sum it all up, I am really unsure what or which sacrifice to credit with it all. He would have no doubt: his faith is stronger than ever, in the sacrifice of Christ on the cross to save a world, which indeed does need saving more than ever,

God knows. Sacrifice! Or as we say in Quebec, "saaa-cree-feeees!"

My father's remarkable reliance on his faith, even through times of trouble, is clear. I once, not that many years ago, checked his library and found only five books not on religion, and those were books I had given him. Both "Faith of my Father" and "My Fake Conversion" show how cocooned I was in the faith, how surrounded and protected. In fact, I think the major remarkable truth that emerges from my account of my childhood in South Africa is how insulated I was from most evidence of the human evil, cruelty and suffering in the land under apartheid. Later I learned, and remembered traces that might have tipped me off: that natives were called "Kaffirs" was clearly, in context, insulting, as it was an old word used only by very old-fashioned, arrogant whites. The dictionary traces one origin of the word to an Islamic word for "infidel," but that sense does not carry the full weight of derogatory connotation as it was used around me then. More telling, I remember that "foetsek," an Afrikaans-based word, was a way to say "go away," "get out of here," to both dogs and natives. But there were no murders or assaults on whites around me that I knew of, and I do not remember any mention of demonstrations against the regime like that which led, after we left, to the Sharpeville Massacre. I only know that my sense was alive, of danger, of injustice, to be awakened later by what I read and heard of the land.

This disjointed narrative is not pleasing to me. I am trying to connect, but the time passed is so vast, and my memory in such limited flashes… But shaped I was by it, introduced to other languages, so that my ear was aware of difference when I encountered Greek, French, German, Quebecois, Spanish, Nova Scotia and other slang…

And in Montreal I gradually became aware of the large number of people with whom I came in contact that had lived for a time in South Africa: Ann Payson, who introduced me to my wife and whose father, a world-champion bagpiper, had taken her there when she was very young, then brought her to Montreal, where her mother died young of alcoholism, and Ann went to Compton School, in the Eastern Townships. Maurice Podbrey, South African expatriate for 30 years, head of the Centaur Theatre, the Anglo (English-language) theatre of the city. My next-door neighbours Alan and Joyce Rose, when I lived for thirteen years on Greene Avenue, who like Ann's father, had gone to South Africa postwar for a time, then come to another Commonwealth country. Alan was an official in the Canadian Jewish Congress; Joyce, born in Shanghai, was a ceramic artist with a kiln in her basement, producing remarkably beautiful work, from small to very large. And the visit, sponsored by me, to my university, of Athol Fugard, a white playwright who organized native theatre when it was dangerous, in Port Elizabeth, in Montreal with his daughter to direct a play at the Centaur. I remember the atmosphere in the room at Sir George, with a third of the audience black but everyone, I think, feeling that fear I had forgotten, of the dangers of living in South Africa. I had a party for him afterward, and his daughter danced with a black man and went off into the city to dance with him, as she could not do at that time at home. We visited his apartment the next morning, and took him to the Grey Cup parade on Sherbrooke Street, in a light snow, with floats covered with plastic to protect synthesizers, etc.

June 23, 2001
In some ways much of the doubt, confusion, and lack of purpose recorded in short notes in the manuscript so far continues. Despite my having published the sixth of the slang dictionaries, and the best to date, *Cop Talk: A Dictionary of Police Slang* (with Aaron C. Poteet, my older son), in spite of having taught an eight-week term of freshman composition at Austin Community College, in spite of having spent near three months living with my 90-year old father and discovering that his loneliness was much

alleviated by my company, his taking care of me, dominoes, and lots of fresh old stories, I recurrently wonder what I am to do. The writing is still a bulwark against despair, truly.

So I press on, a boat against what I perceive to be the current (whether a truthful perception or not).

August 31, 2001

No change. Victor Janoff has been living in my basement here, off and on, for a year. His AA commitment proves to be a weight on my own self-esteem, though he is considerate and thoughtful. But my paralysis continues, and tax troubles, the debt from buying and renovating the house, my aging car and boat all weigh on my mind almost constantly.

Scene One: Nancefield, 1950

My bum hurts a bit. I am sitting on my bed, and Dad did not really hurt me, but he almost never gives me a hiding, and he just did. He must have had a good reason, so I have to figure it out. I am alone, which is what I am most of the time, at home. Dad is busy, with the new church he and the new Kliptown Nazarenes built; Mother has plenty to do, even if Mrs. Cupido does the cleaning. She practices piano every day, and Jim is only two, so she has to change his nappies, clean him, and chase him. Steve and I don't play together much—he's six and I am ten, so I am with other people outside the house only at school and at church every Sunday, Wednesday night, and Friday (for Young People's Society). Melvin Cupido, Sammy Moonsamy, and John Challen are my buddies, but it is Melvin who gets me outside to play cars down in the woods near the river, now and then, like yesterday after school.

I have to think about why Dad took his belt off and gave me six licks with it. I had my school brown shorts on, like all the boys in this hot country. I had lekker not ever make Dad angry with me. Now I remember, the last time he gave me a hiding was way long ago, back in Manhattan, after he saw me sitting between Joycie and Julie, the two cute little blonde girls from next door, and looking at their little ... I don't know what to call them. We did not touch each other at all; I was just curious to see how girls and boys are different down there, and they took off their underpanties. That was before we went to New York to start the long trip in the airplane to come to Africa.

That time, yes, I remember, he said the same thing before he had me bend over: "This hurts me more than it will hurt you." And I could see in his face that it did. I guess he does not want me to get too friendly with girls. It is a good thing he never found out how little Elizabeth, the girl next door at the Bremersdorp Mission Station, cheated on me in the closet: she said she'd show me hers if I ... well, I did, but...

I have to pray about it. Kneel, face down on the bed—there— Dad says God will make it all right and forgive me. Even if I am not sure what was so bad about giving Sarie Marais a tiny goodbye kiss on the cheek when we got to my house. I hadn't noticed her in Mr. Potgieter's big class room before, but today she walked with me from school to the post office, and we got our families' mail from the same window ("Europeans"), and she is cute. She is Afrikaans, black hair and lovely eyes. But I must not talk to her again. I guess Mrs. Cupido saw us ... how she could be looking out the window with all the cleaning she has to do, ik ken nie.

Funny how Afrikaans words come into my head now, like Swazi ones did at Bremersdorp. Dad and Mother think I am a genius for language, so much that I almost believe it myself, but I know I can make mistakes. The one time Dad drove us into Joburg and I got the parking sign exactly wrong ... boy oh boy... We had gone to the American library, and he let me check out a good book, *Praise the Lord and Pass the Ammunition*, which was fun to read. The Bible is full of stories about wars and fights a long time ago. The men used slingshots, like David to hit Goliath, or clubs, like the knobkerries the Swazi warriors carry running along the road in Bremersdorp. In this book the story is about the big American war that was over so we could come to Africa, and the writer is a preacher on board a ship, with big guns. Anyways, I like to talk to people, when they talk to me, and ever since grade one in Bremersdorp, school has been in Afrikaans half the time. Oh, Mr. Wust was Afrikaans. And it is lekker to think how he told me, the first day, that by his old rule he should have to strap me thirty times ... one for every arithmetic problem I got wrong. But he let me off, like God will do if I pray.

He probably would have been angry if he saw me the day I found the drawing of Lady Godiva in the school library. You couldn't see what was between her legs, but it made me tingle anyway.

I feel better. I'll go out and see if Lassie is okay, she is on her chain outside, and Dad says he is going to buy me a Daisy beebee gun to keep bad dogs from making her have puppies. We put her in her cage at night, and she is a good dog. The yard is big, like the house, the nicest one we have ever had. And have we ever lived in a lot of houses. Mother says we moved to Hooker soon after I was born, and I barely remember anything about that little church except that some of the people had Afrikaans-sounding names, like "Loots," then Manhattan for two years, where Steve was born. The war was on, and Dad had a job to preach at the air base, but the house was white, new, and right beside the church, on the street that had lines of big shade trees on each side. Still, this house is the biggest ever. God has been good to us, or at least the Nazarenes, which is the same thing.

Here's the big living room, where everybody at the picnic sang quietly after the boy next door nearly ran over his little sister. There's mother's piano and Dad's solid little bookshelf. He made it himself, in Swaziland, out of some really hard, dark wood, using pegs, not nails. And the floors are nice light-coloured wood, all fitted together, except the kitchen, which has beautiful red paint over the tiles.

Lassie looks fine. She is a good dog, pretty big, but we never have to say "Voetsek" to her, as if she were a bad dog.

I love to look at the orchard, all those apple trees, and the big tall trees along the road.

Oh, but whenever I come out here into the yard, I remember the awful way the picnic ended. There are worse things that can happen to a little girl than a little peck on the cheek! The little Afrikaner girl next door … I was watching, and everybody was, we were all outside in the sunshine, Melvin was right beside me, and we all had cookies and Kool-Aid, and then the noise of the car spinning its wheels, throwing gravel out backwards and the way she tumbled away from the right wheel in the back I thought she was going to be mashed! She was all right, whew, but everybody stopped talking—George

Taylor and Audrey Vanzeeberg and Mister and Missus Pop and everybody—we all went in the house and mother played the piano. And the mother from across the street brought her little girl and sat in the big chair and listened to us sing. And she looked sad and happy at the same time. I think she was sorry her son had lost his temper. He must have been upset to see so many brown people.

John Challen is really black, not brown, and he is an Indian, from Durban—all these people over the line from Kliptown into Nancefield. You see coloureds in Nancefield, but they are by themselves, going to a house to clean it or work in the yard. The houses in Nancefield are all nice, and nobody lives in them except people from England and Afrikaners (I called them Boers one time and somebody shushed me up), and a few Americans like us. Everybody else lives in Kliptown, where the houses are smaller and the stores on Boundary Road, all along toward the church, are all the same, grey. They don't have any electric lights in Kliptown.

Dad's church is for coloureds. They are different shades of brown. The missionaries are "white," not like Kansas snow. We are lighter than brown. In the sun last year for a full day I turned red and my skin was sore and starting to peel. Mother rubbed cream into it to make it feel better. And I would turn a little bit brown, or tan. I know the names of colours from the crayolas, with names like magenta and cerise. My sketchbook from Bremersdorp has a colour map of Africa and part of Europe. Mr. Wust had a machine he called the "hectograph," a waxy top with ink in it. He took my book and put it down on top of the hard wax, and it copied the map onto my page. The oceans and rivers are blue, and you can see the shape of the land. The Free State is orange. Lines show the route the explorers took, like Vasco da Gama from Portugal and Jan van Riebeek, who started Cape Colony.

Anyways, Dad had not planned the picnic to end that way. He loves the coloureds, and he invited all the people who helped him build the church, so they could feel welcome at our house. He had worked with them to build the church. I am too little to carry the heavy cement blocks, but I guarded the water bottles as he passed the concrete blocks down the line to the men with wheelbarrows full of concrete. He looked so handsome, even in a sweat, with his shirt off.

He even brought the mold to make the concrete blocks, Melvin said, and I guess they were all amazed at how good he was at that, as good as he is at talking with people who feel bad.

It is funny to think that when we moved here, last year, I did not know any of these people, and now Melvin and Sam and John are my pals. It all started when Dad and Morris Chalfant, who is bigger than Dad and has a louder voice, held a revival in a tent across from the bioscope in Kliptown. I remember the posters: "Come see the American preacher who can jump ten feet high!" Dad probably thought of that, but he couldn't jump five feet, even. Reverend Chalfant probably could.

A lot of people came to see what was happening in the big tent. I remember how that ended, too. It was Thursday night, and in the big windstorm, I saw the top of the tent start to shift, and before I could pray or anything, the paraffin lanterns were crashing down across the crowd, breaking the glass that shielded the hot light wick or ....mantle, they call it. People were running and screaming. God must have been protecting us, because nobody got hurt, and Dad rented the bioscope on Sunday afternoons when they did not show American movies, so the new Nazarenes can learn how to pray and be good.

Well, I am getting hungry, and Dad won't let me have anything to eat before we have prayers at the table. Especially watermelon, he says after four if I eat watermelon I will wet my bed again, and I do not want to do that any more. I am ten years old now! Dad and Mom say that I walk in my sleep, and I guess they must know, even if I can't remember doing it. I think I may be walking around to try to find the bathroom. I will have to pray tonight to be delivered from that.

Scene Two: Outside Church
A Circus, A Movie, Tuck's Farm, and a British Man on Horseback

Today we had an extra recess at Nancefield School. New and exciting is good even if you like regular class as I do. In class, as I do my work, I watch Mr. Potgieter, too, keeping everybody busy, from the little Form I kids up to the two grades of bigger boys than me. He doesn't run, he sits straight at his desk and tells each group clearly what to do and when, but I learn a lot listening.

No, today at regular recess, Pooksie was shooting his aggie marble straight and hard as usual, taking the other boys' marbles one by one as he hit them. Pooksie is full of ideas, and he tells naughty jokes, but he keeps us busy. He never stops moving at recess, and he squirms in the desk in class. I walked past his little huddled circle as I beetled down to the gates, to buy a can of sweet thick cream to suck on for dessert after the soup and sandwiches.

After that, we had only been back in the big classroom for a little while when Mr. Potgieter got a note from the principal's office. He read it twice, then stood up, and said, "Close your books. We have a visitor. Everybody line up to go out."

The visitor was on a big horse, and we gathered round him like heifers at the gate at feeding time. He had a big tan cowboy hat, and full riding clothes, even chaps and cowboy boots. But when he spoke, we knew he was a Brit.

Funny thing, he talked about his worldwide travels, but he

talked about America the most. The best part was what he said about Chicago, "They drive the cattle in at one end—the stockyard—and they come out the other end in bully beef tins."

Church is not boring, but it is different, more the same week to week. All the services follow a pattern, each one different. Sunday school, Worship, and Evening Evangelistic Service on Sunday, prayer meeting Wednesday, and Young Peoples' (NYPS) on Fridays. Here at school, the British world galloper was the second break in routine since I came to this school.

The first was a movie from America. We knew ahead because everybody's parents had to give written permission, and send a tickey for the movie. Nazarenes weren't supposed to go to movies, but Father said this was special, so I got to go.

Song of the South, the big screen said, with music playing behind. Br'er Fox and Br'er Rabbit were in the stories it showed, with Br'er Fox trying to get Br'er Rabbit into a bramble bush but he ended up caught himself. It's funny, and the screen shows Uncle Remus and his friend talking between each story. The movie was in brown and white, except birds and bees in colour zipped out of the bramble bush and around the patch. Uncle Remus is black, and he talks like Rastus from home, in Texas, not like the Swazis here.

The only other fun thing outside church was Tuck's Farm. Dad drove us there, and inside the gates, the enormous shallow pool—I could stand up on the bottom without getting my chin wet. Old couples, a father dipping his little daughter, and lots of kids were all getting cooled off in the clean green water.

The Transvaal is so hot and dry, Tuck's Farm is like a dream, except you can feel the cool water on your skin.

The circus didn't come from the school or the church. Trucks drove one day past our house and parked on the big vacant field halfway to Nancefield School. I walked down and watched as men unloaded poles and pegs and pulleys. They were putting up the biggest tent I had ever seen. And that was the circus for me, because Dad and Mom would not let me go. I think there were girls on little horses who did not have all their clothes on.

These special breaks in the regular days are easy to remember.

Scene Three: The Monkey Bite

[Not made up—in this book, nothing is—this story also does not represent a turning away from the inner and outer life of my years in Southern Africa as Jarrette, toward the exotic domain, still in existence but threatened, of wildlife. No, as I have said elsewhere, my father did not bring me to the Dark Continent to do safari. He came to save souls, a dubious goal as I see it now, but like doctors who neglect Junior's cough until it degenerates into bronchitis, he not only could not save my soul, but by abetting my schooling in his Bethany (OK) Nazarene college alma mater, he saw me come to doubt that the human animal has a soul (he did not believe that dogs did, and I am sure some of them do). No, this story is about my guilt and ignorance, dark subjects for sure.]

We are leaving Nancefield in a few weeks, to go to Durban, go on a ship, and return home. Dad and Mom have already begun to pack into boxes the things we will take back for the "sabbatical year" there. And my Raleigh bicycle will stay here, in storage, for when we return. Just now Father and Mother have gone into Joburg to get some papers or tickets or something for the trip, and left me to take care of Steve, who is eight years old, small and squirrelly.

Pooksie, the scamp, always full of ideas at school, came by and asked me if I wanted to go visit a friend of his family who has a monkey in the back yard, over in the middle of Nancefield. I've never seen a monkey, in all the five years we've been here. Once Dad took all of us in the 1937 Willys car to Kruger National Game Park, just outside the Swazi border past Mbabane, and I must have seen more than what I remember, which is one giraffe. What a sight *vor myn oog*, tall as a tower, only as far away as from the school building to the gate where the treat truck waited at recess, yellow with black spots, and munching the bottom leaves off a very tall tree. And of course the green mamba that looked at me when I was riding home one day, from the edge of the dark woods, making me throw the bike down and run back. But a monkey here in Nancefleld! I guess I'll go. Have to take Steve along. Pooksie says it is just a few blocks walk, into Nancefield, so it is safe. All white people in these houses.

Well, it was a monkey all right, on a chain fastened to the young eucalyptus tree in the back yard, and looking at us, munching a banana. We looked at it and it looked at us. But when it dropped half of the banana on the ground and then ran back to the other side of its circle, who knew that Steve would be curious and want to give it back to this little *skellum*, this little monkey from the jungle?

And when he picked up the little yellow treat and held it out to the monkey, he was inside the circle of the chain, and the monkey scampered over and in a flash, bit him on the leg! I don't know what to do. should tell Dad and Mom, but how can I? We got back to the house before they did, and I'll get a hiding from Dad, for going without leave, for sure. The two little round holes the monkey's teeth made on his left leg just under the hem of his shorts are small but… They did not bleed. I am not going to say a word.

* * *

It's been a month since Steve got the monkey bite, and I had forgot about it. But Dad preached more than once on "Your Sins Will Find You Out," and he was sure right.

Plenty to distract me from this guilty memory. We are the

only passengers on the S. S. *Ruth Lykes*, passenger cabins on each side, captain's deck, enough to hold twelve but we are only six, and we have the two on the starboard side, since we are Father, Mother, me, Steve, little Jim and baby Dewey.

I loved seeing Table Mountain—flat flat, flat—as we chugged and churned around Cape Town, which I had never before seen, *niemals ersten gesagen*, no, *gesehen*. Dad had made a trip down to the Cape Colony area, to preach to the Cape Coloureds, who are a big part of the people there. In fact, I guess Melvin and Mr. Pop and the other coloureds in our church in Kliptown must have all come from there, farther back among their grand and great grandparents. But for once, he did not take me.

Then there was the ocean, as we turned toward home, blue, cold blue, not like the warm Indian Ocean, which was brown, and had some jellyfish in it. I found out on the beach at Durban the first time we went there on vacation, while we still lived at Bremersdorp, because I got a small sting on my back. It went away, the mark it made, not like Steve's bite.

Because yesterday, Steve's other leg, his right leg, swelled up and I had to tell Dad about going over to see the monkey without telling him, and the bite. Dad did not whip me with his belt, because they were so worried that Steve was poisoned. How could the poison shift from one leg to the other? It was in the same place on the other leg. I worried because we had no doctor on the ship, only Captain Boy, the mates, the engineers for the huge motor to drive the ship, and all the crew, ABs and OSes (Able-Bodied and Ordinary Seamen).

One of the ABs, named Whiskers, is becoming my friend. He liked me enough to break a ship's rule: he took me down into the engine room and all the way along the big slowly turning shaft, big as a tree, to the circular stair up to the aft lookout at the stern. But the Officer on Duty on the bridge spotted us, and I guess he got a talking-to. I wouldn't have missed that adventure for anything, even though the engine room, deep in the middle bottom of the hull, was pounding noisy, smelly of grease and oil, and full of sweating working men.

We must be quite a different sight for the men, breaking into their ordinary days and duties. Dad goes down and has coffee with them on their breaks. He told me that once he asked one of them if he found the coffee strong, and the man said, "Do you take it straight? We put half water in ours!" But they all came on one sunny Sunday morning out on the foredeck and listened to Dad preach and try to sing "Rescue the Perishing," with mother playing the accordion.

Captain Boy gives me a cold Coke from his fridge, every now and then. The first time I wandered up to his private sun-deck, curious, just exploring, I peeked from behind a stanchion and caught him nekkid sunbathing, but I ran back to the cabin before he saw me, not making a sound.

Then there is Sparky, the radio operator, who showed me how the ship knows always what direction to go. It is a big round metal and glass thing on a set of hinges, "swivels," he calls them, and it is a "gyroscope" or a "compass," or something.

Also, and this is the best, he is teaching me how he sends messages. He uses a clever new language, not like Swazi or Afrikaans or Zulu, but using English words and spelling. The difference is that he taps his "key," a finger-thing that makes dots and dashes in a radio sound, and he calls the language the Morse Code. He calls the dots "dits" and the dashes "dahs." So the distress call, SOS, is dit dit dit dah dah dah dit dit dit. I have learned all the letters and numbers now, and I practice them with my fingers on my right knee, because I don't have a key or a sound machine or radio. But Sparky said I could buy a cheap Morse Code machine, a transmitter, from a discount house in Des Moines, Iowa, and a receiver, a Hallicrafters S-40B, and the transmitter kit would be easy to put together myself. Or just a little "crystal" set, with a long antenna wire on the roof of our house. I am going to try to do it, if I can get a paper route or sell some calendars and Christmas cards like I did in Nancefield, door to door, and make a little American money.

And Whiskers has promised to buy me a banana split, with loads of ice cream, when we get to New Orleans, because I have never tasted one. Mmm.

It's a good thing I have all these things to look forward to, because I felt so bad about being bad and letting Steve get bit by the monkey. I even went on feeling bad after I prayed about it every night. I want to be good, I really do. The Nazarenes have so many rules, but God is merciful, the Bible says, to sinners. And I guess, I must be one.

P.S. Oh, yes. I almost forgot to tell you about another stupid and silly thing I did. I am not sure whether I am smart or not. Maybe I am like Mother, smart with words and music and not like Dad, smart at making things. Dad made the church, even making the concrete blocks with a mold he rented, and then showing the people how to put them together when they got hard, drying in the sun, to make the walls. And he made a super book case, which he brought with us on the ship, taken apart and stored in a box. It has three shelves, of dark African wood, with pegs instead of nails.

Mother and I are quicker than he is with languages. Mother learned Zulu really well and fast, with a little book she bought, and I learned it and Afrikaans perfectly, just listening to people talk and imitating them. I sing and play some on the piano and accordion, and she even plays on the portable pump organ, for street meetings. Dad can sing some songs in Swazi, but not in perfect tune and without knowing what the words mean at all. He had to have a translator when he preached in the bush in Swaziland.

Anyways, after we left Cape Town, and all we could see that was not on the *Ruth Lykes* was water, water everywhere, I decided to try to get a little of it. So I kept a paper cup from the mess hall, and Whiskers gave me a roll of string. Without telling anybody, feeling like I was doing something naughty, just naughty, not sinful, I tied the string through two holes in the side of the cup and threw it over the side from the lowest deck that was open, at the middle of the ship. How stupid can you get? Of course the wind carried it away, broke the string and tore the cup, and so I did not manage to get any salty water to taste. I had better stick to words and music, pray (in three languages) and sing (same). But maybe I can make myself a radio set.

Oh, Steve recovered from the monkey bite. Captain Boy had a medicine kit, and I guess he fixed it up, and Steve was all right. Thank God. I have never understood why the infection was in the same place on his other leg.

The monkey was smaller than Steve, and quicker.

His tooth marks were even, on Steve's upper left thigh. Even, like the eyes of the green mamba stared into on the gravel road three years earlier in Bremersdorp.

But the snake did not bite me. The monkey bit Steve.

But now I wonder, as with Leda after the swan's quick, shuddering come in her loins, since W. B. Yeats wondered whether she put on His knowledge with his power…? Did Steve "put on" something from the monkey, from his bite?

Steve got very quick, in the few years he had left, until the day in June 1963, when the blood-leak caused his skull-base to swell, in the arms of his lover in his bedroom at 2501 San Antonio Street, in Austin, Texas. Then he stopped moving his body at all.

Two South African Ladies

The last five days of my 2012 return to South Africa I stayed in Tremeton House on the business school campus of Witwatersrand University, in Parktown, Johannesburg. From this bare-bones one-room (plus kitchenette and bathroom), Melvin fetched me to visit Kliptown, I sallied forth into Braamfontein for Skype and cellphone time-purchases, and on the last day crawled about with a sore knee to pack for my flight home.

Closer to downtown than to the airport, it was my spot from which to be in and see the Joburg burgeoning, teeming pastiche, the horn of plenty. Plenty of people, garbage, money, poverty, colour, traffic. Rolling hills and freeways. Warned that danger lurked, I did not take out or open my cellphone on any nearby street, made friends with the guard-post men at both campus exits, and never went out alone after dark.

Well, I did take dinner the last two nights at Mike's, a fine restaurant a half-block up from the main campus guardhouse, but I walked fast in the dusk and even faster back after wine and the ample, tasty feed. And it was at Mike's that I met Dixie and her partner Jocelyn Nightingale.

Mike's Kitchen (Parktown) is in one of the two grand old houses left from when it was the Randlord district. Guarded by tall cedar hedge-trees, three solid stories high, with Cape wines, it lured me back a second night.

That night was the end of the school year, and several tables had a family around a blazer-and-tie clad lad, Father in work shirt, mother and girls suitably simp and twee. But in the tiny bar, Jocelyn gave me a hard, narrow-eyed stare as I took in her girlfriend, florid and loquacious Dixie.

I glimpsed them only because after my solitary, sumptuous dinner, I had glanced in the small bar as I floated back to my table to pay up, and saw the two women. "Someone to talk to," I thought. Back at the table, my waiter, seeing my next move, seemed to stammer as he tried to caution me not to hit on these girls, because ... well, you know, "they do not much like men."

Dixie, better at asking questions than listening, is a clinical psychologist, educated at the University of the Witwatersrand, and dressed in full colour, flowing skirts and big hair. Jocelyn, butch for sure, wears denim and talks directly, makes sense. And she warmed to me, unaccountably.

It started as soon as I sat down with my wine bottle and a glass from Bobo Dhlamini, the bar steward. We were three points of a triangle, facing each other, Jocelyn sipping Scotch neat, Dixie with a Pink Lady. Dixie leaned toward me and asked "What was your first memory??" and "Are you comfortable in your body?" and finally, "Do you think you need some psychotherapy?" I had dodged and weaved and parried, but now I snapped, "Not now. Not here." Jocelyn laughed, and broke up the sweet, tipsy interrogation—"Let's have a smoke." As we shared a cigarette on the tiny balcony, she told me that she had gone into banking in the early 1990s, was from the Cape (returning next day by seventeen-hour bus for a Christmas visit), and wanted me to call her next morning so that we could wish each other "bon voyage," her home to the Cape, me home through Heathrow to Montreal.

Most of what I say came non-verbally. In her tone and in what she did not say, I knew that Jocelyn had seen the horror, and worked hard. Her face was eloquent beyond words, of years of struggle, of achievement, survival, and triumph. Her strong mind. Her driving will. Her good heart.

She was taking Dixie for a princess ride, and when she gave

me a sisterly, cousinly hug, I said, "My ex was briefly in your lesby-friend mode at Wellesley. Take care of that beautiful girl."

We spoke on the phone the next morning.

In the afternoon, a car nudged me onto the hard surface of Jorissen Street, cornerways from the WITS art gallery. Sore in my left leg, I took taxi back to my room and packed for home.

Appendix
Key Words

As my central focus in language has been with words, specifically slang words, I provide this list of the key words on which I build this project.

VOETSEK or -SAK. An Afrikaans term shouted at a mean dog chasing you, "Go away!" A "footsack" would impede the dog's running, but that is not the source of the word. It is Afrikaans for the Dutch "voort seg ek," "Forth! say I." (*Dictionary of South African English on Historical Principles*, Oxford, 1996). Some Afrikaners hurled voetsak at black people, with the same meaning, but a racial insult. "Voetsek, you smelly beast." To the Nationalist Boers, blacks were not fully human, meant to obey, keep their distance, and to be punished by lash or bloody death if they were resistant to the divine mandate that gave the land to the Afrikaners. Both Transvaal and Orange Free State were declared republics, separate from the abandoned British-dominated Cape, after the Great Trek by the Voortrekkers, which has been called "the world's largest moving prayer meeting" (Michael Cassidy, *The Passing Summer*).

BOSBERAAD. "A discussion in the woods," literally "a woods council." Held in utmost secrecy, literally in a forest, between men only, who came from all sides of the Nationalist apartheid/African National Congress divide. The signal bosberaad in the early 1990s lasted until a break was reached in the deadlock/

standoff and was the final step before the release of Mandela, the unbanning of the ANC, and the free election. Before that crucial bosberaad, newspapers noted several called by F.W. de Klerk, with only his cabinet ministers present, and one journalist suggested they were for "secret hushed-up lobotomies."

MISSION, MISSIONARY. Name of the incursion of Christians (Nazarenes, Methodists, Anglo- and Roman Catholics and others) into the black, coloured, and Indian cultures of South Africa. This word is nowadays as taboo as calling blacks "bantu" or "hottentots" or "Kaffirs," or calling Afrikaners "Boers." The main word replacing it is "partnership."

TRANSVAAL. Former name of the most populous provFince, around Johannesburg, now known as "Gauteng," or "place of gold." Many place-names changed after 1994. Afrikaner and British names, e.g. Pretoria became Tshwane (the local tribe), and "Orange" was dropped from the name of the former Dutch Republic province to the south of Joburg. But not all, as some heroic martyr place-names like "Piet Retief" were kept. In the new Republic, "Dingaan's Day" was named a national holiday, for the great Zulu chieftain warrior. In a comic vein, a newspaper reported in the fall of 2012 a village's protest to try to keep its name, which in Zulu means "the virginal thighs," because the people honoured a chief who, they said, actually had very shapely legs. ("Hands off our Chief's Virginal Thighs?") "Natal," containing Durban, was retained with the prefix "KwaZulu." The current president, Jacob Zuma, is a Zulu, but clearly no Luthuli (Zulu chief, and associate of Mandela). Unlike Zuma, Mandela never played the black card to the denigration of Afrikaner, British, Indian or coloured citizen population. He insisted on keeping "Springbok" as the name of the national rugby team, when hothead vengeful blacks wanted to change it (see the Clint Eastwood movie *Invictus*).

N.B. The key words I have listed above are not a complete list, but are alike in that they are very rarely seen in print. "Voetsek" or "Voetsak," is exemplary. A tabooed word which was also extremely common, it bears the marks of shame earned by its use as a racist invective epithet, a weapon in name calling. "Missionary" is also virtually an "M"-word among Nazarenes of my acquaintance today. They call their efforts "partnership," meaning they ask what parents of schoolchildren will do to supplement money given for roofing materials, either through work on the project or giving food or money. "Bosberaad" does appear in most dictionaries and word-lists, but without usage examples, and the crucially secretive nature of the event seems to hang around the word. "Transvaal" and many place names are more visible, to help people like me who followed the disturbing and then hopeful years leading to 1994 without noticing that place names had changed.

CLAN NAME. In print, much more evident now that apartheid is no longer a bloody daily reality. Nelson Mandela includes his Xhosa middle name at the beginning of his autobiography ("Rohilhlahla") as a signal of this change; the familiar name by which he has always been called, "Madiba," is his clan name, and it became the affectionate term with which to address or refer to him after he was released from Robben Island (throughout *Invictus*). In another context, during Mandela's three-week hospital stay, Jacob Zuma, trying to stay presidential in the public eye despite a vigorous press attack on his alleged greed and graft, and even an allegation by a rival politician that Zuma could actually not read, made sure to trumpet the name with which Mandela, Zuma said, greeted him when he reached the ward to escort the 94-year old national hero out of hospital; "He shouted my clan name, "Nxamala, as I walked in."

NKOSI SIKELE AFRICA. Name of the new national anthem, replacing the Nazi-like Afrikaner previous one, "Die Stem." Important not just because it is in a black language rather than Afrikaans, but because each of six verses of the song is in a different tribal language.

TOWNSHIP(S). Usually refers in the 21st century to a shantytown which is a poor and often dangerous black settlement, near a large city, often on the outskirts. However in 2012, in the valley surrounded by upscale Hout Bay, in Cape Town, a new shantytown is creeping along the slopes near the valley bottom, fed by refugees from both within and outside of the Republic of South Africa. In the 1950s, a white residential centre would be known as a "burg," since, along with "dorp," it was the Afrikaans word for "town," and a "township"was always nonwhite, usually supplied water only at outdoor pumps, and was the site of burning tires in the streets at night and the risk of violence. The white area near Kliptown where my family lived from 1949 to 1952 was called Nancefield, and I never heard it called a "township." Now that area is all "Soweto," an acronym for South Western Townships.

Also, among names for living areas, "location" is another. In the 1940s, a "location" was a nonwhite African dwelling zone with a buffer, and portable, as whites kept nonwhites at a distance, but close enough to serve as labour. The government wanted control. Trevor Huddleston (Naught for your Comfort) defines and describes a "location," but notes that Sophiatown was never one. The root, "to 'locate,'" has two meanings, both about control: if you locate ("find"), you know where they are, i.e. it is intelligence; and if you locate (or "re-locate,") you more than know, you choose, dictate where exactly they will be,especially at night, so you may make arrests and keep order (or lose it if they riot).

N.B. The main language besides English spoken by almost all white South Africans and many blacks and coloureds, "Afrikaans," has a history which bears directly on the keyword list. The word itself is derived from the word "Africa." But just as Afrikaners may be known precisely and proudly as "white Africans," their language was a homegrown hybrid. Descended from Dutch (but Afrikaners do not like being called "Dutch"), it is so larded and intertwined with English that many words in almost any sentence are partly clear to a non-speaker. One Nationalist party campaign slogan for the retrograde 1948 election victory was "Die wit man moet altyd baas wees." Only the last word might be problematic for a beginner from English to understand. "Die" is "The," "wit" is "white," "moet" is "must," "altyd" is "always," and "baas" "boss." In Germanic word order, the last word, the verb, is the verb "to be," which is "werden" in German. So: "The white man must always be boss."

Moreover, Afrikaans was "created," according to reliable sources, by the prominence and energetic effort of the first religious leader to serve the new Dutch colony after the 1674 Jan van Riebeek landing on the Cape: it was not a parson from Holland, but a Scottish "dominie" named Murray, the only available spiritual guide to show up. He was accepted and influential because the Dutch Reformed and the Scottish Old Kirk and other Presbyterian faithful worshipped and lived in a fervent, stern Calvinist discipline that was virtually identical.

BLACK, WHITE, COLOURED. It is not only the skin colour that identifies one as black, white, or Coloured. In Nancefield in 1949 the post office had separate entrances and separate windows for "European" and "non-European." At the height of apartheid, living areas were designated for whites or nonwhites; even moving around a city or the country required nonwhite people to have a pass. Some beaches were reserved by signs for "persons of the white race." In the Southern U.S., a spatial gulf also existed: back of the bus. Now, in South Africa, persons of any colour mix freely in public and private. But among street people, black and Indian beggars are invariably neatly dressed and clean. White ne'er-do-wells are the most pitiful, filthy, ragged human jetsam adrift on the streets. In hotels, guests are of any colour, but serving people are invariably nonwhite.

BLACK SPOTS. Poor land to which, in Natal, Indian people were forcibly removed, from homes in Durban, especially, according to Michael Cassidy in *A Passing Summer*. A government action known as the Group Areas Act generated some of these displacements, but the forced removal of nonwhite South Africans was a recurrent Nationalist Party tactic to take land desired by the whites and to destabilize the opposition. Nelson Mandela records the resistance, futile in the end, to the destruction of Sophiatown, not merely a residential area but a burgeoning artistic community; he and Winnie were moved to Kliptown, as was John Challen, of a Hindu priest family, from another neighbourhood close to the centre of Johannesburg. The common experience of blacks, Coloureds, and Indian South Africans was one uniting influence that made the ANC coalition come together.

Notice these keywords; they lead to a set of themes, buried but key links between parts. Themes, say, like apartness versus joining together; love versus hate; brethren in harmony versus brethren in disharmony; then versus now; Lewis (observer) versus others (Swazis, Coloureds, Indians; women and girls; missionaries; Afrikaners; Zulus; Xhosas—the real subject of the project, as distinguished from the "observer," who is just a lens).

Postscript

Writing after, embracing these fragments, I follow the narrowing path for deepening certainty laid out since Kant, who said we can never know the thing in itself (*ding an sich*). Then the Romantics felt locked in the self, only sure of how it felt. Kierkegaard could only be sure that he, and he alone, existed. Even the Victorian Julia Margaret Cameron, an early photographer, fingered focus as a variable technical term of rough measure: "Who has a right to say what focus is the legitimate focus? [Rejecting the 'definite focus,' hers was best reached by stopping when 'something to my eye was very beautiful.']" (Joan Acocella, *New Yorker*, September 2, 2012).

In our time, the problem is this: to give the reader something the reader wants, you must take him where he wants to go, a place he is curious about, and you are the only one who can take him there. But then there are no corroborative witnesses: "I alone have escaped alive to tell thee" (Job).

So: be truthful and detailed. And find a consistent, believable voice. Then tell the story.

Lewis-Jarrette Poteet

I was born in Oklahoma

I grew up in Swaziland and Soweto (Nancefield, P. O. Kliptown)

I did school in Hobbs, TX, Bremersdorp, SZ, Nancefield, SA, Bethany, OK, Norman, OK

I finished school in Minneapolis

I married in Ohio, fathered in Minnesota, moved to Montreal

I worked at Sir George and Concordia

I weekended in Island Brook, summered—sailed, canoed, swam, gardened—in Nova Scotia

I reaped words in Nova Scotia, and all over North America

I fetched more words in Renton WA, DFW, Farnborough, Paris

I moved around in Montreal: the Pointe, Montreal West, Snowdon, Laval/lac, Roxboro

I loved Susan, Jackie, Cassie, Ronnie, Tanya, Carla, Karen, Martha, and ... and ... and ...

I published in Hantsport, Halifax, Montreal, and Bloomington, IN

I launched in Montreal, Chicago, Wichita, Austin

I sailed in Port Latour Bay, Cape Negro Bay, Barrington Bay, Shelburne Harbour, Lakes of 2 Mtns and St.Louis, up and down the Ottawa and St. Lawrence Rivers, in the Seaway down from Gananoque

I retired from Concordia, and from Discount Car and Truck rentals; and from driving motor vehicles

Dogs were my friend/pals—MacDuff, Alvie, Burrito (a.k.a. El Chapa)

I culled and discarded in Westmount, Snowdon, Laval, Roxboro; I renovated in Roxboro, where I gardened, cooked, wrote, sang, drank, walked, bicycled, scooted (briefly)

I mended in Reddy Memorial, Lakeshore General, Montreal General, CLSC Pierrefonds

I traveled in Heathrow, Tambo, Durban, Manzini, Parkdale, at WITS Business School campus, Schiphol

I repented and rejoiced inside my body and with my spirit

CAST A COLD EYE
ON LIFE, ON DEATH
—Horseman, pass by

Epitaph on the gravestone of W.B. Yeats, from his poem,
"Under Ben Bulben"

Lewis J. Poteet
Curriculum Vitae
"What I have done so far in my life"

When my father brought us back to the U.S. Southwest after five years as missionaries in South Africa, he was invited every weekend to travel to Nazarene churches from Washington state to the northeast, and in almost every state of the Midwest, to tell of his experience overseas and to raise money for the missions. He brought me along, and I was asked to speak to the Sunday school classes. I was twelve, but here first I composed words into true stories and spoke them. At thirteen, I had a suit and an invitation to hold a week-long "youth" revival in Tucson, AZ. I rode to the job, a first-time boy "preacher," in a driveaway car from Dallas. I returned on the bus. In my 3–5 spiral notebook I wrote outlines for the sermons I delivered at each of the ten services, number in the audience (total for the week: "26 seekers."), the cash take for the week ($101.33), exact expenses on the trip (net take $62.70)—a clear instance of small-time "Capitalism and the Protestant Ethic," eh?

When I entered Bethany Nazarene College, my parents' alma mater, I was a religion major, and studied New Testament Greek the first two years. Early my junior year I switched to philosophy, and, falling asleep in the library, moved into English. M.A., Oklahoma; Ph.D., Minnesota; Associate Professor, Concordia University (1973–1998). I was in freshman English administration at Minnesota and for three years at Sir George Williams University.

My first slang dictionary, first of twelve, was called *The South Shore Phrase Book: A Nova Scotia Dictionary*. Alone or with a co-collector, I published slang samplings on Quebec's Eastern Townships, hockey, cars, planes, and cops. I read and published papers on historical, aesthetic, and anthropological issues arising from the raw material I collected. I was the Canadian contributor to the revision of *Partridge's International Dictionary of Slang* (London: Routledge, 2006). One entry in the South Shore book generated a story in Macean's; Robert MacNeil and George Elliott Clarke used my book as a lexical source to flavour MacNeil's first novel, *Burden of Desire*, and the poems of George Elliott Clarke. Radio interviews came with Gzowski, and Montreal and Halifax CBC.

In retirement, I first signed on for winter eight-week session teaching at Austin (Texas) Community College, where I could visit with my aging mother and father. After their deaths, I spent six years as a contract driver for Discount Auto Rentals in Montreal, gathered material for the *Partridge Slang Dictionary* revision, and served on graduate committees for some students in the thesis stage.

I am writing again.

My Books

The South Shore Phrase Book (Lancelot Press, 1983, 1985, 1988, 1990; Nimbus, then iUniverse, 2004–).

(with Aaron C. Poteet), *The Hockey Phrase Book* (Eden Press, 1987; Lancelot, 1991; Robert Davies, 1996; iUniverse. 2003–).

(with Jim Poteet), *Car and Motorcycle Slang* (Pigwiidgeon, 1992; Robert Davies, 1997; iUniverse, 2000–).

(with Martin Stone), *Plane Talk* (Robert Davies, 1997).

(with Aaron C. Poteet), *Cop Talk* (iUniverse, 2000).

My essays: a score and more, over 100 pages, on topics from Oscar Wilde, Alice Munro, and Maria Chapdelaine to hockey, aviation, and Maritime slang, on to the ownership of stories, graffiti, and South Shore Nova Scotia oddities such as a cult from Tennessee that moved into Barrington, renovated an old schoolhouse and ran it as a successful restaurant, and a summer outdoor theatre troupe in Shelburne.

Notable Essays

"Romantic Aesthetics in Oscar Wilde's 'Mr. W. H.,'" *Studies in Short Fiction* (Summer 1970), Vol. 7, No. 5, pp. 458–464. Over ten years later my chair pointed out that this was called the best thing ever written on "Mr. W.H." by an Irish bibliographer.

"Whose Story is that anyway?," *Matrix* (Spring 1991), No. 33, pp. 59–61.

(with Jacqueline Baum), "Rough Measure in Maritime Dialect Research," *New York Folklore* (1987), Vol. 13, No. 3–4, pp. 105–111.

Grants Awarded

Freshman Scholarship, Bethany Nazarene College, $200, 1957–1961.

Graduate Fellowship, University of Minnesota, $8000, 1966–1967.

General Research Funds grant, Concordia University, $1500, 1987–1988, for research in the Eastern

Townships preparatory to publishing *Talking Country: The Eastern Townships Phrase Book* (Pigwidgeon Press, 1992).

General Research Funds grant, Concordia University, $650, 1993–1994, in support of the airplane slang project resulting in *Plane Talk* (with Martin Stone; Robert Davies Publishing, 1997).

Brothers in History, Brothers in Time: Henry and Frank—Melvin and Me

The three people most important to my experience of South Africa are my father, Henry T. Poteet, my colleague Frank Chalk, and my boyhood friend Melvin Cupido. Although no two of us are blood brothers, my father said to me a few months before he died that "in heaven" he and I "would be brothers." With that word-leap he set me on this tracing of the intangible but real parallels that the four of us share in our lives in time.

Though they never met, my father and Frank Chalk followed the academic discipline of history in very different ways; though Melvin and I were out of touch for over half a century, when we met again as adults, in November, 2012, we discovered that our lives in time were parallel in many ways.

The branch of inquiry known as "history," like every one of the great ways of shaping our piecemeal visions of our world, is different for each of its pilgrim servants. It was my father's major subject at Bethany Peniel College. His favourite professor, Fred Floyd, a stout, dignified senior faculty member when I knew him (1957–1961), fixed his mind mainly on the Civil War ravages inflicted on his homeland, Old Dixie, by the Union general William Tecumseh Sherman. Dr. Floyd was from Georgia, and Sherman's slash and burn "march through Georgia" both ensured the Union victory and sealed widespread Southern hatred for the North.

Dad acted, though, on a very unhistorical spur, his dream one night in 1944 Kansas, a dream in which black people waved and called for help. He also confided to me a secret bit of family history which shaped his destiny and ignited his dream. His father, Lewis Cass, before walking at age seventeen from Missouri to Texas, had impregnated a black maid, begetting upon her a son (illegitimate, a "git," as they say in Nova Scotia) who died in infancy, who would have been "coloured," and who was named Henry. "I wondered if I was fated to die early, too," he told me. So he followed these signs, his dream and the family secret, to South Africa.

In the first three years he was put in charge of the mission farm at Bremersdorp (later renamed Manzini), Swaziland. Having left the West Texas Poteet farm to go to college and then into the ministry and the mission field, he was surely disgusted to be slotted as a farm boy, or in this case, farm boss (in that place, "baas"). Where the Poteet homestead in Fisher County had been 400 semi-arid acres, a "section," the Bremersdorp farm was 400 "morgans," four times larger, but more land and even more fertile land would not have reconciled him to the change from what he saw as his dream-fulfilling mission. On my follow-up trip in November 2012, finally finding Dr. Samuel Hynd near Manzini, I knew that the week spent searching for him had been worth it when he responded, on hearing my name, "Poteet! This clinic is built on the land at the outer fringe of the farm your father ran."

Running the farm did not satisfy his dream. Clinging to his call to save African souls, Dad once commandeered a surplus World War II weapons carrier he found on a vacant lot in the mission station, and with a tent, drove with me into the bush, the "outback," put up the tent, and held services for any who would come, for several days. Never fluent in Swazi, as Mother was (I have her *Lessons in Zulu*, annotated in her fine round hand), he had a native translator, Dhlamini. And in his Pastor's Pocket Record, begun in western Oklahoma, he gives details of his other preaching assignments. An entry for a service always includes such sermon topics as "Sowing and Reaping," "The Quality of Eternal Life," or "Your Sin will Find You Out."

He unfolded the Word at various places around Bremersdorp. Many were at the Bremersdorp Court House, many at the Boys' Hostel, some at Bremersdorp Coloured (a school), Mustapha (now the industrial town between the capital Mbabane and Manzini), the "Fick house" and several identified only as "North of Home (7 kraals), and North by the Mountains (8 kraals.)" A "kraal" is a Swazi native family compound, arranged like a "corral," as the two cousin words suggest in their sound echoing. The "kraal" events are clearly "calls," or pastoral visits, not services; he also gives over a few pages to dedications and baptisms. By 1949, he is in the Transvaal, and then the entries cease—he was too busy planning the Kliptown tent-revival to write anything in the book.

So the lasting, tangible work Dad did in the last three years in Africa was very concrete. Literally. In fact. I learned when I returned to the church that he astonished the new converts who were helping him: he brought a mold to make concrete blocks, and they cast them and built the small dark brown building, with steeple, that stands today. The ceiling is still the original pressed tin. I remember exactly how they passed the building blocks down a line of men, Dad in the middle, as the walls of the church rose block by block, row by row. It sticks in my mind's eye, Dad, sweating, working in the line with the men of the young church, but I did not know about the mold until the current pastor, Lloyd Solomons, told me how surprised the men were at Dad's practical choice of this specific tool.

And now came the big surprise of the whole trip: sixty-two years after he built it, the Kliptown Nazarene Church is making a bid to be named an Historic Site. Young Rev. Solomons said that other Soweto churches more prominent in the anti-apartheid movement were fast-tracked for this distinction. As Lloyd spoke, I marveled inwardly that two key links between the church and the movement had just been given me, so that my writing could help speed the process along. Ten years after his death, I have a chance to help him take a small place in history.

Henry Poteet and Frank Chalk never met, their paths to and away from history were different, and where Dad was spare in frame, Frank carries the dignified build of the professor, keeping fit by early morning runs wherever in the world he awakens. They are put side by side here only by my having been guided by both of them in my exploration of Africa. When I prepared to return, to write about the changes in that land, in September 2012, I first phoned Frank, professor of South African history at my school, Concordia University. Always active, not a thought of retirement, teaching, working with the Genocide Centre he co-founded, and regularly travelling to conferences, he was at the same telephone number as when I retired fourteen years before. In the first of two hurried two-minute calls, Frank gave me a month's worth of essential reading (Mandela, Antjie Krog, Coetzee), a video link to a speech by conflict resolution scholar Heribert Adam, and the names of two pertinent recent films (*Winnie* and *Searching for Sugarman*).

So Dad moved from dream to action and back into a mystical mode. Near the end of his life, he asked me for books by George Macdonald Fraser, the late Victorian fantasist, and Frances Scott Burnett (*My Secret Garden*). Frank Chalk, never religious that I could detect, is constantly busy in think-tank world conferences on genocide prevention and conflict resolution. The day I left Johannesburg, he was at a two-day conference at the University of Pretoria, a few miles to the north, to which I was probably inadmissible—the speakers and panelists were retired World Court justices, generals from all over the world, other professors. Both my Dad and Frank pursued, along different paths, their different readings of history to try to make a better world. But they shared a focus on Africa, and an unshakeable conviction that all humans have the same worth and deserve the same chances.

Melvin Cupido, my closest friend when we were ten, drove me to Kliptown. When I looked in the left front side window of the Benz, he beamed at me with his familiar Alfred E. Neuman "What, Me Worry? expression on his smiling round face. As we caught up on the sixty years since we last spoke, we marveled at what parallel lives we had led. We each have fathered two sons. Though he dropped out of school after the primary grades, and I continued through the doctorate, both of us had keep the King James Version of the Bible in active memory space, from which we quote regularly, sometimes seriously, sometimes in scoffing jest, through years of drinking, gambling, and substantial involvement with many adult female friends and lovers. He had reformed himself (his fiftieth wedding anniversary was just before Christmas, 2012), through an *Illuminati*-schooled vision that sees time as an illusion; the human body and indeed the entire visible material world as property temporarily rented, copies of the divine originals; and world leaders (including Mandela, Obama, Lincoln, and the Queen) as "devil-worshippers," on the grounds that they work actively in the world of material, money, and temporary political power and, oh yes, have links with the secretive Masonic Lodge. He had rejected any conventional view of the world in favour of the *Illuminati* vision of contemporary history. I regard crop circles and *Illuminati* lore as a sort of cult. But he saw what I needed and where he could take me. And he did.

Melvin and I, eagerly tossing out memories as we drove into Eldorado, talked of Sammy Moonsamy, who had helped us find each other. But Melvin asked whether I remembered the fourth of our little band. "John Challen," he said, "'challenge' without the 'ge.'" I did not. Melvin phoned him anyway, without explaining to me, so that I was surprised when later he met us at the church.

As we neared the little brown church my father had created in 1948, its shape was exactly as I remembered. At the base of the steeple tower, I leaned over and brushed the grime of time off the cornerstone, until I could make out the words on it. "Alvin H. Fortner Memorial" it read, barely visible through the dust of sixty-four years, and I knew I had come back. I could not help it: I gushed happy tears.

John Challen, a retired Nazarene pastor by this time, was Indian, his skin colour ebony black. He clearly remembered me, but I saw why I had not remembered him: he was a bit younger, and my eyes were on the two older friends, Melvin and Sammy. But John's story linked the Kliptown church with antiapartheid as no other could.

His grandfather and father both Hindu priests, John came to Kliptown amid hard times for his family. Forcibly removed from the city as Mandela and Winnie had been from Sophiatown, they had trouble paying for his school. One night in a rainstorm, with no street lights, the eleven-year-old John Challen made for the brightest light on Boundary Road. It was the paraffin lantern outside Dad's church. He entered, was touched by George Taylor's sermon, and went to the altar.

"Where is the little curved altar now?," he asked Lloyd. "It was at that end, then. My tears are in that altar."

His life was changed, and with the education the Nazarenes supplied, John had married, preached, and retired in his new world.

"It was the Americans," he said, "who brought us the Gospel. The Afrikaners never did!"

As for me, after the intervening years of a life so like Melvin's, I have forgiven and rescued myself, with the help of poetry (specifically Yeats' "Dialogue of Self and Soul") and am at work on the in-time memories of my life. They are fragmented but vivid, and my joyful work is to take the sorry, often bloody, sometimes lovely and hopeful disordered mess that is my bit of history, and look for rescue for us all. Like Obama, I suppose, a foolish dreamer, I keep alive a hope that rescue may come, somehow, some day.

That is why I write. This book is as true as my eyes see. It is as accurate as my mind remembers. My left eye is 20/40. My right eye is 20/200.

My two living blood brothers were both born in South Africa, but neither has so far returned there. Other brother Steve, who grew from age two to eight there and then died in 1967 on a motorcycle west of Austin, Texas, never spoke to me about the place. Likely he did not remember much, or more likely he was too busy living in the present to spend time on our past. But sticking with the "brothers in heaven" kinship that Dad foresaw for him and me, Melvin is clearly a brother. We cannot choose our relatives by birth; we find brothers (and, of course, "sisters,") through common ground, common goals, sharing and warm feeling. But just as brothers do not always agree, even fellow Christians may differ widely one from the other. As I began to explore the Afrikaner Nationalist years, precisely when I read the detailed story of the absurd kangaroo court trial of Mandela and 150 other anti-apartheid leaders, I began to doubt my ability to be even and fair-minded with the ruling Afrikaner government men, despite their fervency of Christian faith. So I began to consider examples of the unbrotherliness of some brothers (and sisters).

Brethern Dwelling Together in Unity (Not)

Behold, how good and how pleasant it is for brethren to dwell together in unity.
—Psalm 133, verse 1

The most dramatic and effective sermon I ever heard was preached on this text, and it was not to a crowd of hardened sinners. No, it was at a camp meeting in rural western Kansas farmland, two years after our return from South Africa. En route home alone from a preaching gig, I took a layover on my M-K-T (the "Katy") railway ticket, and was in the crowd of Nazarenes under the tabernacle roof to hear the special speaker. In his native England, he had lost an arm in the World War II German bombing of London (the "Blitz"), and as he unfolded the Word, he used his left white, stiff, artificial arm to punctuate his British-accented speech with dramatic gestures, chopping the air at key moments for emphasis. I was so dazzled that for years I misquoted the verse as I mimed the gestures. "How beautiful [right arm sweep right] upon the mountains [added by me—left ARM chop up] it is for brethren [left ARM chop down] to dwell together [left ARM sweep left] in harmony! [left ARM joins good right arm in grand sweep]."

Rising to the occasion of this spiritual (and spirited) performance, seasoned greying preachers wept and moved down to the altar at the call. What they were confessing down there on their knees, God only knows. In my fertile, horny, naive little fourteen-year-old mind I could only imagine, from the fervency of the feeling, that it must be some secret sexual sin, say, schtupping the servant à la Schwarzenegger. Of course here I was just projecting my own secret physical sin trap, my nightly fall from grace as I helplessly, obsessively played with myself under the covers and then, every night, did the repentance ritual. On reflection, they were more likely responding to the exact message of the text and the sermon, and feeling keen guilt over some minor envy of a neighbor minister friend who had been preferred for some boon they wanted for themselves, rivalries which did not exhibit perfect love, or maybe the fetching flash of a housewife caught answering the front door in her nightie, eyes averted but not quickly enough not to notice that her underpanties are red. The Tenth Commandment is specific and detailed: "Thou shalt not covet thy neighbour's wife nor his ox, nor his ass."

So as I come to write about my boyhood perceptions of disunity and disharmony among the missionaries, the various Christian churches of various names and passions and agendas, and even the problems in finding the necessary unity among the diverse foes of apartheid, this text leaps out as an ironic title for these stories of unfortunate, deplorable, divisive, retrograde interactions. Of course the moments or decades of unity, the meetings where power and sustained peace and friendship, or at least acceptance of the other, came to life—these must be seen and told, too. But the glitches are easier to see than the successes, and I remember them longer.

On my 2012 return trip, not a week into my ride up the Indian Ocean coast, the local newspapers in the East Cape and in Swaziland offered hilarious proof, with brighly colored picture, of an event at a Methodist church in Mazizini village, near Port Elizabeth, that God's children in Africa are not yet united in perfect love and sweet smooth fellowship. The headline, "Hell breaks loose at Methodist church," under a picture of red-clad, white-hatted, scowling old biddies, opens a news story of a Sunday morning melee which saw guns drawn, and display and some use of knobkerries (hand-carved clubs), sjamboks (whips), pongas (machetes), and knives. The conflict had to do with which faction owned a church building, plus the renewed appointment of a controversial bishop. Police had to send the faithful home to prevent bloodshed.

In Swaziland the Anglicans consecrated the first-ever female bishop, just as the mother church voted once more to delay its permission for such revolutionary action. And in Mugabe's liberated African republic further north, his pet bishop issued support statements for the dictator he had blessed, disregarding the police cat-and-mouse raids on anti-Mugabe Anglicans who wanted to worship in their own churches. They are currently meeting in alleyways, basements, and under bridges. The Nazarenes regarded their own occasional "persecution" individually and as a fringe group, as a sign of God's favour, a mark of purity, some kind of divine test, or Pop Quiz from the God who knows everything already. My reading, too, thrust before me the bitter division, for scores of years, between the Dutch Reformed Christians who saw apartheid as a key part of God's plan for them, and the often Christian anti-apartheid forces. Thus for years the avowedly Christian Methodists, Anglicans, Nazarenes, Zionists, and Catholics were joined willy nilly with some comrades who were card-carrying communist agnostics in Mandela's remarkable, hard-won, common action (the African National Congress) joining blacks, coloureds, Indians and liberal whites. The Dutch Reformed church refused to withdraw its support for its Nationalist government when pressed by the World Council of Churches, which in turn threatened to eject them. They withdrew from their worldwide faith community rather than see the light and change direction.

Of course divisive splitting and separating is common in Christian history, with the vaunted One True Church, the Roman Catholic, sprouting Anglican and Orthodox Catholic offshoots; Methodists reducing the Thirty-nine Articles (of faith) to twenty-five, only to have the Nazarenes come out from among them with twelve; and Matthew Arnold shaking his head over a proud sect that ballyhooed itself as "the Dissidence of Dissent, and the Protestantism of the Protestant Religion." Even other faiths split and fight: Sunni and Shia, Hasidim and Reformed in the religious state (Ysrael) that has never been able, by 2012, to elect a majority government.

The first story I noticed as a boy, of this "How sweet it is when Brethren...," this irreverent mishmash, comes from the first year in Swaziland, at the two patriotic celebrations that happened apart but both within the first week of July. The Bremersdorp missionaries from the U.K., led by Dr. David Hynd, OBE, CBE, feasted under the Union Jack on Dominion Day, July 1; the Americans countered with an Independence Day fete on July 4. Though very few of us were so gung-ho as to hum "I was born at the feet of Old Glory," the Second World War had aroused our nationalist pride. The Brits, many of them actually Scots, were more low-key in their celebration, by hearsay. We never invited them to ours; nor they us to theirs. I can only guess that they at least toasted King George VI, who visited Swaziland in 1939. If Dad was anti-monarchical, it did not show when he took me to meet Swazi King Sobhuza, who wore the colourful native costume for the occasion, and did not address me directly.

Our regular connection with the church in the United States (the "Kansas City headquarters" of the International Church of the Nazarene) was a radio broadcast called "Showers of Blessing," the time zone difference, eight hours, so remarkable that we had to set alarms and listen to shortwave radio in the wee hours, every week. On the Voice of America, an energetic, unctuous quartet sang the theme song—"Showers of blessing/ Showers of blessing we need/ Mercy drops round us are falling/ But for the showers we plead." The British, with only a two-hour head start on Greenwich Mean Time, must have had a way to relieve homesickness in those days long before Skype and cellphones, so David and Agnes Hynd may have rationed themselves to the once-a-year Christmas message from the reigning monarch.

At any rate, Dad made no close friends among them. His pal Jim Graham, an Irish tenor who first sang "Danny Boy" to me, standing by mother as she accompanied him on the piano, was from the U.K., but he was no Limey; he was an Irishman. Because I did not then know the difference, I mistook Dr. Hynd for an Englishman because of the O.B.E. and C.B.E. after his name. His son Samuel finally laid that one to rest in November of 2012. The founding doctor, his father, was born in Perth, and one of Samuel's own two medical degrees was from Glasgow. In fact, the Scots had been the first of the Nazarenes to arrive in heathen Swaziland in the 1920s, years before the American Harmon Schmelzenbach forded rivers with donkey carts in the thirties.

And to go boldly, deeply, into my family closet, I must say I am sure the conflict between Dad and Doctor Hynd, which ended in the crushing of Dad's missionary dream and sent him into a month-long emotional whirlpool, this enmity must have fed on Dr. Hynd's very correct and accurate perception of an American foolish impulsiveness in Dad. For, you see, Dad apparently made a public accusation that the good doctor was reserving white patients for himself and sending blacks to his American understudy, Dr. Laurence Seaman. Whether it was true even once, let alone as a practice, I shall never know; but its crude naivete, to say nothing of his own resulting hurt pride and anger, moved Dr. Hynd to lead a campaign among the field missionaries during our sabbatical year to marshal votes against Dad's return to the mission field. Dad lost by 75 percent against, the most massive rejection on record.

When the news reached my father, in mid-furlough year, he went to appeal in Kansas City in person, doubtless crying, "I had a dream!" It failed. The mission board did not restore his remaining half-year of travel and fund-raising in the most prestigious niche known to his church ("returned missionary"). So he came back to our lodging in his old college town, Bethany, Oklahoma, went into a room, and for thirty days fasted, cried, and prayed. Mother, menopausal all of a sudden, went free wheeling in her head, causing Dad to be angry with her the only time I ever saw in their sixty-two-year marriage. He called her "woman," and mimed a slap at her face; I went all Oedipal inside. Dad was out of a job, and when a friend gave him a month's carpentry work in Duncan, in Southern Oklahoma, we moved there briefly and I got my first paper route (*Duncan Daily Banner*. Duration: one month. Net pay total: $0. I was cleaning up the book for the route, and when I had it done, we moved again.)

The downward spiral of Dad's life seemed to take a short updraft when he was named pastor of the church in Grand Saline, Texas, and I could mow the huge lawn beside US-80 west and share my lips and nimble fingers ("necking" and "tit-groping") with, in turn, each of the two Nazarene lasses my age in the church, Jerry and Evangeline Sansom. But that church voted him out too, and after one more shot, in the Cedar Hill suburb south of Dallas, Dad had to find other work. At the end the Cedar Hill Nazarene flock owed him back salary, and so we shifted to a rented house in adjacent Duncanville, just moved onto a muddy lot and still on blocks. Dallas First Church gave us a "pounding," a public gifting of canned Spam, wieners, and beans and Melmac cups and plates in the church basement. It was kindly meant, urgently needed, and hugely embarrassing. Dad then failed the Ling-Temco-Vought aircraft template shop qualifying course, blew an encyclopedia sales gig (he sold one, and took a used typewriter as down payment in lieu of cash), and spent a few weeks refinishing used pianos, working in nearby Irving for George Story or Storey, a shady friend with an alias used only in Tennessee.

After a few weeks at the Dallas Sanitation Department dump counting loads of garbage, Dad took a master's degree in counseling in Denton and became a sixth-grade teacher and school advisor. To the end of his days, he still had some supply-preaching, but his cash came from counseling in Duncanville and Taft, Texas.

Not even the motorcycle death of brother Steve in 1967 so wrenched my father's heart and spirit as this abrupt blindsiding dead end. Dr. Hynd, on the other hand, must have felt he was excising, surgically to be sure, a festering, divisive sore in the body of missionary Nazarenedom in South Africa. The missionaries had to be unified and together to be an effective force for God. In a world in which religions are divisive, Dr. David Hynd was trying to be a uniter.

When brethren identify people not their blood kin as brothers and treat them as brothers, a link is attempted that may bring healing unity into our troubled world. During my return trip, the *Johannesburg Star* (November 22, 2012) printed a full-page story about one such effort. A colour photo shows a white man in saffron and ochre Buddhist robes addressing a group of black women and children in an open-sided outdoor rural tabernacle in northern KwaZulu Natal. For ten years the man, Gen Sandak, of unidentified national and cultural origin, has been teaching Buddhist compassion, "calming [of] the mind, and meditation," to bring peace to people who need to recover from "illness, trauma and violence [that have] for generations been part of daily life." Not seeking to convert or build personal or religious empire, Sandak works at the invitation of a community leader, Patti Joshua, of the Senzoguhle organization in the Eshowe region north of Durban.

Also in Johannesburg, the first South African black billionaire, Patrice Motsepe, pledged to give half his wealth to charity, joining Bill Gates and Warren Buffett in the "Giving Pledge" (*Forbes* magazine as reported in the Toronto *Globe and Mail*, January 31, 2013). Born in Soweto, where Dad built his church, son of a woman who gave food to poor customers at her small grocery and a father who was banished to internal exile in Hammarskraal for "criticizing apartheid," this eighth-richest man in Africa says "South Africans are caring, compassionate and loving people It has always been part of our culture to assist and care for less fortunate and marginalized members of our community."

Looking for any religious or church roots in Patrice Motsepe's life, I found the web of his affinities complex. A clergyman from Zion Christian Church, Barnabas Leganyane, is an associate, so there probably were evangelical strains and influences in his upbringing. Many others situate Mr. Motsepe amid the "black diamond" power elite of the post-Mandela African National Congress, which current South African president Jacob Zuma heads. Clearly some of the success of Motsepe's African Rainbow Minerals corporation has to do with his close ties to those with power, from Edison Power Group and the Eighth Zulu Monarch to an ex-wife of Zuma who was born a Dhlamni (the royal family of Swaziland.) As Mr. Motsepe has been credited with funding one of Zuma's lavish four house-estates (for which Zuma was accused of paying with government money), he may be seen to be part of a rescue-put-out-the-fire campaign by Zuma. Nonetheless, the pledge harmonizes with Ubuntu, the "traditional African philosophy of humanity and generosity to others," and is a new trend in "philanthropy," so long considered a "domain of white missionaries and churches." As a weak world economy makes it hard for any state to spend freely for even much-needed hospitals, roads, and schools, Motsepe is in the avant garde of a new inclusive strategy to improve the lot of poor brothers and sisters.

"The real barbarity starts," writes Alexander Marine, to introduce his stage version of Coetzee's *Waiting for the Barbarians* (1980), "when we begin to divide people into 'us' and 'them,' based on the colour of their skin, their religion, their political views or simply because 'they are not like me.'" Maurice Podbrey brought a South African troupe to perform this play at Montreal's Segal Centre in the winter of 2013, as he had brought dissident playwright Athol Fugard to the Centaur a score of years before.

In the brotherhood of affinity, Dr. Samuel Hynd, since we met face to face in late November of 2012, seems to me to be my older brother by inner kinship. This eminent physician, 88 years young and running an AIDS clinic outside Manzini, took time to drive me around on the two following afternoons and talk with me. Without knowing what he was giving me, he said at one point, "When Chief Luthuli took refuge from the Boers, he was given shelter here on the Nazarene mission station." My head snapped around and I began scribbling, for Luthuli was President of the ANC before Mandela. Born in Bulawayo, Rhodesia, he was a missionary son brought to Natal at age 8. Congregationalist, he believed that "the road to freedom is via the Cross," and he used his 1961 Nobel Peace Prize money to buy two Swaziland farms to provide havens for political exiles (WITS University archives). The brother ties between Zulu and Swazi, between Coloured and Indian, between Dhlamini (Kings of Swaziland) clan and the Nazarenes, are main anchors of my belief that my father's church was a strong, quiet force against the evil of the fifty years of apartheid repression.

My brother Samuel, son of the man who cut my body to heal it and helped cut short my father's dream, gave me that nugget of historical truth amid his stories from age five about watching the ox transport of the stones given by the King for the Nazarene church and the toy cars with which he and the District Commissioner's son played in the yard of the British emissary's house, as he let me off in that spot, now the parking lot of my hotel, the George.

Brothers in history. Brothers in time.

Anybody's Army

For years I have said, at least once a year, that I do not join anybody's army. The possibilities include the Nazarene (the Army of the Lord), the U. S. miltary (in 1966–67, I was classified IIA, both father and graduate student deferments, during the intensifying Vietnam war draft), and I never publicly joined any organized protest event against the war, though I did not want to serve there,and believed it to be a criminally evil war for oil. If I had been drafted, I would not have refused, and I believed I would have been slotted to work in intelligence, as a code clerk or translator.

Despite this show of bravado, I was briefly a cadet in Boksburg school at age ten (see the picture with the oversize Eisenhower hat that falls down almost over my eyes). On my return to the U.S. at age twelve, I eagerly joined the Boy Scouts in Bethany, Oklahoma, trying to "fit in," and barely managed to ascend one rank above Tenderfoot, to Second Class Scout, earning merit badges for language and the God and Country award. To get the latter, I washed windows at the back annex af Bethany First Nazarene Church and picked up garbage along Route 66, which ran through the centre of town. Also, I joined the Brotherhood of Railway and Steamship Clerks, Express Handlers, and Other Station Employees, when I worked two summers for the Texas and Pacific Railway. I was a vacation replacement clerk. I was saving money for college, as my father had no money to give me. Finally, I was part of the narrow victory that won the right to have a union of professors at Sir George Williams University.

This union was part of the huge Quebec Federation des Travailleurs du Quebec.

The street-sidewalk garbage collection in Bethany was a one-day event, but it had permanent results. While I was in the eighth grade in Bethany, I put on my Scout uniform, took a garbage bog, and began picking up scrap paper, pop bottles, etc., on the south side of the highway opposite the college I would later attend. People would ask me what I was doing and offer me a coin, which I declined. Shamed, the city council put in garbage cans the next week. There were very few cigarette packages, because downtown Bethany was unusual in that no tobacco or alcohol was ever sold there. Written into the deeds was a provision that if any merchant dared to sell them, his title would revert to the city. Bethany was as far outside Oklahoma City as the original Bethany in the Bible was outside of Jerusalem, and my cousin Peggy Ellis Poteet has described the town as the Nazarene "Mecca."

I was still not a part of anybody's army.

I acted alone.

I lost my Nazarene faith at Bethany, driven out by narrowness and hypocrisy, and attracted by the great world of books, art and music, colour, sex, and sin. I become a troubled, angry non-believer. But recently, with the good example and influence of my cousins Jim and Peggy at the college, and the Nazarene effort to send the gospel light to Swaziland in the concrete form of solar water pumps, I have begun to rebuild a sort of faith. I will never again be a Nazarene or even a Christian. But I am finding a new humility, a reverence, and a belief in some realities that cannot be explored by logic or science. I am drawn now by a search for beauty, for grace. I am a sinner and a pilgrim, and I am profoundly grateful for the events in my life that have led me to this place.

(Written at the George Hotel pool bar, December 12, 2013, at 7 p.m., the first and only writing I have done in South Africa.)

My Escape from the Nazarenes Graduation Day, 1961, Bethany Nazarene College

As I fold my black B.A. robe and stow it in its box, in the Bresee Hall cloakroom, in comes Dr. Forrest Ladd, psychology prof whose courses I never took. Tall, rangy, lean, he shows kindness in his face, as always. He listens, rarely speaks first. But now, he does.

"I hope someday you like us better than you do now."

Holy Christ on the Cross. He can see inside me.

"Us," he said. As he leaves, I place the box in the rack, my last act before I leave this place, forever.

I never thought of him as "us" with Cantrell, the unctuous old fat patent-fool president of the "college." Or with Snowbarger, the executioner of Board orders ("kick Poteet out") last spring. Dr. Ladd is a good person. As are Dr. Harold Hoyt, Dad's classmate in the '30s, now a religion prof. I had gone, just last year, to his office to seek relief from my continuing guilt (like indelible ink, guilt lasts longer than faith) over the physical delight I could reach with artful manipulation of my choad by Peter Palm and his five sisters. He tried, for once, nonreligious sensible calming. "Actual sex is not all that exciting," he claimed, weakly. "Sure," I thought, and left.

Now I am out of here. My mock repentance worked. It's only thirty miles across the southwest corner of Oklahoma City to Norman, the University of Oklahoma, and I'm already registered for a full load of summer courses, starting next Monday.

The great world, free of Nazarene blinders, Sooner Cinema, the Campus Tavern, across the street from the Student Union north exit. I'll be there. I rented a room from Mrs. Adams, on the street bordering the west side of the campus, and she made me chortle inside. From Mississippi, widow of a business professor, she said, "Didjew evah read thet Willem Faulkner? He useta set around all day, nekkid, typing."

I barely remember the despair of last June, keeping the Snowbarger bust pent up inside me for a month, straightening out the files at Ace Auto Air Conditioning on Highway 77 South. The siren lure of an exit from my pain in a flash: the car coming fast, one quick dash, the end.

Recoiling, I finally told Dad, who went to the BNC Board, got me readmitted on probation.

Just now the feeling of release is all I have room for. Never mind deep sadness at the loss of that cocooning close warm safe feeling of my years of prayer, self-abuse, and nightly repentance. I have already told Brother Neilson not to renew my preacher's license. I said it quietly, and his face, as kind and understanding as Dr. Ladd's, was just a touch sad as he nodded.

Free at last, thank godamitey, I'm free at last. If anyone seems not to know the Nazarenes, I help them, mutting through my teeth, "Jim Jones' first church."

2010. Lunch at Forrest Ladd's, Bethany
In the solarium on the south side of the house, we sit around the table, Forrest, his wife, his daughter (now an English professor at BNC or SNU or whatever they call it now). Lunch is fresh and tasty. Sun is bright. We are relaxed. But I have a question I've wanted to ask him for a quarter of a century. "Do you remember what you said to me after the graduation, in the cloakroom?"

"No, I do not," he says. "Tell me."

"'I hope some day you like us better than you do now.' Time is supposed to heal, but I am still as angry as I was that night, even as I miss the faux comfort of the life of faith. Is there a way to explain that, the persistence of a lasting, unstoppable hatred?"

"Teachable moments can embed themselves in us for a long time," he offers. I half listen, but this idea, this inward human process, freezing a mind-set, a soul-set, like the shutter of a camera, capturing a moment entire, which then is impossible to change, makes sense to me.

Forrest Ladd seems so bright and educated and kind that I am astonished to learn that he had been a preacher.

Sex, the Swazis, and the Nazarene Saviour

The Bible says it clearly: "Be ye fruitful and multiply." But the Nazarenes seem to have been confused about how to obey this rule, because they were hysterically afraid of sex. Dad went into a fit of fear whenever he detected any interest in me in what boys and girls, husbands and wives, birds and bees might do to follow any strong impulse to get naked and do what comes naturally. He took off his belt and gave me a spanking, muttering "This hurts me more than it does you," which seemed to me an obvious untruth.

His best friend in South Africa was Jim Graham, a single missionary from Scotland who had been brought to the "mission field" without first marrying: the rule was marry, and then the couple would come as a new missionary team. Jim came to our house for dinner a lot and after dinner, in his classic tenor voice, standing beside the piano he would sing "Oh, Danny boy, the pipes, the pipes are calling/ from glen to glen…" with the lovely refrain "O Danny boy, I **love** you so." LOVE is not exactly SEX, as we could tell in church," where we sang "Love divine, all loves excelling" … and it did not mean erotic love, but Agape, the love of God.

Sixty years later, Dr. Samuel Hynd told me about the Nazarene policy, from which he himself had been exempted at first, and explained that it was so that sexual interest, strong in men, could be controlled by being purified by marriage. Dr. Samuel had been needed urgently to back up his father at the hospital, but he had returned to Scotland and married a London girl, who came back with him, bore his offspring and then died tragically, crushed by a small car left in gear and parked over a drop-off in his father's front yard. The car reversed when she started it.

Jim Graham had become engaged to a Miss Flitcroft, a nurse from the U.K., who shortly thereafter fell into a flirty friendship with the married Mr. Shirley, the American printer (not their real names), and both of them were put on the first available plane home, and Jim went to Tanganyika to heal his hurting heart. (He married another nurse, and served out his whole life as a Nazarene missionary with her, in what became Tanzania).

Swaziland seemed a natural place for the Nazarenes to wrestle with the world, the flesh, and the devil, because the Swazi people were extremely fond of two of the major Nazarene sins, beer and sex.

Indeed, Mary Douglas, an anthropologist who studied their ways, said to me after a lecture in Montreal that she was frankly puzzled that the Nazarenes ever attracted any converts there. AIDS went stupendously, cruelly wild, wiping out an entire generation of breadwinners, until Dr. Samuel's clinic and other rescue operations got hold of it with effective control drugs.

And in my own case, nature trumped the Nazarene prudery and policy and prayer. May as well confess that my poor confused body, virginal until I was twenty-two and figured out what to do with a sixteen-year-old chubby cutie in a Sunday school class I taught at Dallas First Church who had shed all her clothes in a one-hour rented bed in a West Dallas motel, and eagerly welcomed my breathless attention, then asked me with a smile whether her tampax would fit in easier. Bless you for not the most romantic of words after first fun, but for some of the sweetest words I heard in my life, anyhow. (The other hilarious verbal event that afternoon came from the black room clerk who accepted my money, craning his neck to look at Dad's 1951 Ford where she waited, and said, "Oh, I see you got your own girl awreddy.")

Can't blame the Nazarenes for my ten years of masturbation, nightly repentance, and subsequent lifelong obsession with the Heavenly Gate that every female in the world carries around for making men merry: it was Dr. David Hynd who had taken a scalpel to the most sensitive spot on my body and made it hurt so bad for five days that I gave it loving attention for ever thereafter, and whenever I could, let it take wet, wild, wicked joy in a close bodily encounter with any willing woman. There it is, in the Old Testament, with many examples: "AND HE WENT IN TO HER/ AND HE KNEW HER. Bless the Lord, O my soul, and all that is within me./ Praise his holy name."

In 1958, when I was in my second year at Bethany Nazarene College, scandal broke when the pastor of Oklahoma City First Church, R. T. Williams Jr., divorced his wife to marry the wife of his music director, who then, newly divorced himself, married the former Mrs. R. T. Williams, Jr., and all four of these horny sinners moved to Southern California and became swingers who never darkened the door of any church ever again.

Where Was the Secret Meeting? (BOSBERAAD)

Near dawn in London, December 16, 2013, and I am finally having a coffee Americana, costing £2.70. Returning from my last research trip for this book, I am at the outer ring in Heathrow Airport, beyond baggage pickup and security, lower level. Just outside the automatic doors are the bus and tube access platforms, and just before that final set of exit doors, to the right, the first "smoking permitted" area, with one bench and the "wheelbarrow" sculpture garden, about thirty yellow and thirty green. Sitting in the little drizzle, this sculpture garden is so striking I have to look at them first, even in the dawning dark daybreak.

Before I ordered this coffee, I had limped out there for the first smoke since Joburg Tambo airport yesterday, a full fourteen hours ago in elapsed time. My swelling feet, dizzy head, my irrational panic, made this the worst flight so far (out of seven, last year and this), but British Airways Special Services eased my trek for a fag, whizzing me and other gimps and oldies in in the little electric trolley deep underground through elevators, concrete corridors, in ten minutes moving me where my first time I had walked for an hour. Fast through the checkpoints, priority, head of the line—no, in fact, through the crew checkpoint where there was no line. My very first time, on November 7, 2012, I walked for an hour before I found fresh air with which to dilute the nicotine smoke, and my feet were tired. I had only stopped once, to ask a guard, "I see these little green exit signs, a running stick figure above the word 'emergency.' If I really, really want a cigarette, is that an emergency?"

So I have no complaints. That car that nudged me last year onto Jorissen Street and started the battle with my lower body should be thanked: I had a fortunate fall, even with pains and panics factored in.

As I settle in to the padded low sofa, and put my coffee cup and saucer on the table facing the window, I remember that I may buy a newspaper a few steps back toward the baggage exit, and I will be able to pay with a Canadian $20 bill, and get sterling in change. The man I just asked said, "Certainly, you may use any money anywhere here. We like anybody's money," with a chuckle. I grinned, but inside I thought, "Sounds cosmopolitan, but they still keep the pound, and shun the euro. So all these other moneys get converted into the old British money, and I bet they make a tickey or two coming and going, every time."

In this little nook, there are at least four seats, and I am taking up one, so I am not surprised to see a well-dressed couple settle in opposite me. After a bit, as I always do, I greet them, "Good morning," trying to sound "South Efrican."

"And good morning to you, sir," the husband responds.

"Where to today?" l ask, prepared for anything from "Hamburg" to "Hong Kong."

"We're just here to pick up our daughter," the wife volunteers. "She flies in from New England."

"Oh, not far from where I live, Muntreeall," and I relax, someone to talk to.

After the usual explanation, my 1946 beginning in Swaziland, the sixty years away, the two trips back, the project, I mention that the one detail I have not pinned down is where exactly the bosberaad, the secret meeting, took place, to free Mandela.

Unbelievable, what comes out.

The man looks directly at me, and says, "Our friend Michael Young arranged it. It was at Henley on Thames, not far from here, the first meeting, and then for a week, at a private estate in Somerset."

My eyes tear up as I write this, the fulfilment of my impossible hope, that I could find what no one has put in print, at least in print that I have been able to cast my eyes over, yet. Indiana Jones, Lewis Jarrette, that's you, with your "research vest" that people are always taking for a fisherman's rig. Hell, no, it is not the grace of god. It is what I believe in, that the random passing of facts and colours, lies and truths, to the alert mind and eye, produce blessed luck. And for that, over and over for fourteen months now I am profoundly grateful.

I have a scoop.

Of course, it may not be true. I shall ask Dr. Jonathan Pons, but he is so busy that unless I make this expensive and taxing journey back, to ask him face to face, I may never get denial or confirmation from him. I check Catherine Bradley's *Causes and Consequences of the End of Apartheid* (1998), and it has nothing. The Toronto *Globe and Mail* front-page story about South African doctors in Canada (December 6, 2014), quotes Johann Malan (same family, different politics) who, when he was the young military doctor caring for Mandela in 1989, was summoned to accompany Madiba as he was transported to the "secret negotiations," but he does not say where they were.

Funny, isn't it, I reject the Nazarene faith, with its absurd naivete, as I see it (Dad thought the Six-Day War was Armageddon), but I believe this stranger and his story, because it has the exact answer to my biggest question. At least it is specific. And let's turn one of the believers' word-tricks right back in their face. "Something cannot come from nothing, so there is a God, and I am going to tell him what you said when I pray next." These optimistic believers actually are "sure" not only that there is a God, but that he, she, or it controls the universe, especially mine, and that they have a Red Telephone directly to him. *OK, buddy: the bosberaad was in England, got it? If you can't disprove it, I gotcha.*

It makes good sense. England had the empire during the nineteenth century, and the Commonwealth provided a link that worked well when Queen Elizabeth leaned on Ian Smith to get out of Rhodesia. Cecil Rhodes' day had come and gone, and the Rhodes Scholarships, a good force in the world still, do not legitimize a white government over black people. Even Mugabe's tyranny is better, for he has the right skin colour to let him try to correct the course of his country in the new Africa. Likewise, when the country at the tip of the continent has run itself into what looks like unresolvable dispute, England may atone for its abdication of responsibility there, leaving the Boers to drive their misunderstood mandate through the bodies of suffering non-white people. It did so by using its faded grandeur and glory to lure the deadlocked men, Boer and ANC, criminal police and communist, and sit them down comfortably until they agreed and allowed the light to shine, the light of Freedom, Justice, and a better future.

An Eyewitness to Black Schooling and Life in a Pretoria Township in the Late 1930s

From Es'kia Mphahlele's Down Second Avenue *(1959), an African career toward writing very like mine:*

On my first return trip in 2012, at the WITS University bookstore in Braamfontein, I bought the book, and did not notice how it echoes my own patterns until two years later. Now, to fill in the dark unknown zone just before we arrived in South Africa in 1946, here are some flashes.

At school, where Es'kia was dutiful and alert:

> Boys in the upper classes often said Big Eyes's caning [the headmaster wore glasses] was nothing compared to his predecessor's. We heard stories often of how that gentleman used to buy sixpence worth of firewood, put it on the floor, and order a boy to lie on it for caning. It was crude firewood with splinters and knobs sticking out, so that if the boy tried to move because of pain, the wood pricked him to a more or less stationary posture.

Notice the irreverent use of the Old Testament story.

Es'kia was careful in his behaviour, but his anger sometimes makes him talk back:

> I was walking with two friends, also Pretorians [near the good school outside Joburg], along the left curb but on the tarmac. Two whites on a motor cycle came tearing down in the opposite direction. The driver came straight at us and we jumped on to the pavement.
>
> "Voetsek, you Boers," I shouted impulsively.'

He is disciplined, gets just a talking-to by the headmaster for this insolence; the headmaster tells him that the powerful whites may close down the good school, if he protests in this way again. Eventually his school, St. Peter's Anglican, south of Joburg, is closed by the Anglicans rather than submit to the Bantu Education Act.

The school taught the Black Man that he could be equal to a white man.

Finally:

> I decided not to go to church any more. The white press, the white radio, the white Parliament, the white employers, the white Church babbled their platitudes and their lies about "Christian trusteeship"—"the native emerging from primitive barbarism." Secular institutions wrenched the pulpit from the Church and cited the Scriptures. While the white preachers told their contented suburban congregations the story of Calvary and individual salvation, white churchgoers felt committed to group attitudes and "white supremacy."
>
> [In 1948] ... these white people voted to Parliament a bunch of lawless Voortrekker descendants whose safety lies in the hands of Sten-gun-happy police youngsters.

www.ingramcontent.com/pod-product-compliance
Lightning Source LLC
Chambersburg PA
CBHW060608080526
44585CB00013B/731